MOMENT

OF CLARITY

Cover art:
Jami Sherman Triplett

Photography:
CS Muncy
www.CSMuncyPhotography.com

Design & typography:
Fearless Literary Serivces
www.fearlessbooks.com

Printed in the United States of America

Lee Camp

M+O+C BOOKS

NEW YORK

Contents

CONTENTS

CONTENTS

CONTENTS

CONTENTS

CONTENTS

Introduction

When I started writing humor at age 13, I couldn't have known I would become a stand-up comedian. When I started doing stand-up at age 18, I couldn't have known I would ultimately make my comedy about world issues and cultural commentary. And when I started "Moment Of Clarity" on February 1st, 2011 — a short bi-weekly rant which often revolved around the corporate pillaging of our nation and the world and the collapse of a meaningful life — I couldn't have known that the Occupy movement would explode into our nation's zeitgeist on September 17th of that year. The same anger and frustration that fuels Occupy fueled many M.O.C. episodes even before Occupy began. The first M.O.C. to attract the attention of tens of thousands of people was "You Are Not Alone" in which I say,

> *...You are not alone. There are millions of us who can't see a future in the way things are going, who regardless*

of political affiliation are — first and foremost — anti-corporate ownership of our society, and who are willing to stand up to let it be known.

In May David Degraw, of AmpedStatus.com, asked me to participate in the first attempt at Occupy. I agreed and created a video promoting the June 14th "Move Your Money" action. The action called for people to withdraw their money from the big banks that continue to screw regular Americans out of every dime and dream we have. It was to be done in coordination with an occupation near the NY Stock Exchange. I made a video entitled "Top Ten Ways To Punch Big Banks In The Nads" (I always use the most sophisticated language), and I moved my money out of the big bank I had lazily continued to use for 10 years. Unfortunately the occupation did not take — but like a rash, we would flare up another day.

On September 17th we tried again, and a few hundred protesters gave birth to Occupy Wall Street. The energy down there that first night was amazing. Those of us who had been screaming about this stuff for months and years finally watched as America woke up. Besides just being a participant in Occupy Wall Street I got the opportunity to perform stand-up comedy at Zuccotti Park as well. To watch my live performance, go here:

http://youtu.be/gaFdla-F2GM

Although screaming from a wall on a drizzly night with no microphone to 1,500 people is not the ideal scenario for a comedy gig, that performance was like nothing I had ever experienced. It truly felt like we were sitting on the crest of a wave that is a consciousness revolution. I went on to perform and/or protest at Occupy DC, Occupy Chicago, Occupy Asheville, NC, Occupy Milwaukee, Occupy Toronto, Occupy Ohio University, Occupy Madison, WI, and Occupy Montreal. Each one was different and alive in its own way. But they were all the same in their mission — bring this world back to the people over the corporations and the wealthiest 1%.

In the following pages, you'll read the transcripts of roughly 90 Moments Of Clarity. Some have important messages, and some are more hilarity than revolution, some more desperation than evolution. Some are meant to create debate, and some are meant to end it. I've kept the transcripts here nearly identical to the words first spoken in the videos on my website (LeeCamp.net). Occasionally I changed some wording — usually just to make it easier to understand or grammatically correct. However, you will quickly notice that these "rants" were never meant to be written down. They're written the way I would speak them. There are many sentence fragments and run-on sentences. I didn't change most of those for this book because I want them to read in your head as I said them in the videos. Comedy is very much in the timing — so I hope you have your game face on. You're about to become a comedian.

This book is dedicated to the millions around the world who have stood up in the past year. Some have died, some have been pepper sprayed, some have been arrested, some have been detained indefinitely like Private Bradley Manning. I've had friends arrested for chanting, dancing, tweeting, and sitting. And others have been beaten in the head with police batons. But in the end, the unimaginatively wealthy who defend the ravaging of this world will have their money, but as the band The Darlings say "we'll have a soul."

The Mayans said the world ends in 2012. That's because another world is possible.

Keep fighting.
Lee Camp

PS: At the beginning of each chapter of this book, you will see a URL just underneath the title. That's where you can find the video version of each chapter. If you get a chance, subscribe to the Moment Of Clarity videos at

www.YouTube.com/LeeCamp2

Moment Of Clarity is also a twice-a-week free podcast available at www.LeeCamp.net, on iTunes, at Stitcher.com, or as an Android app. Guests on the podcast have included Janeane Garofalo, Greg Palast, Chris Hedges, John Oliver from "the Daily Show," comedian Stewart Lee, The Yes Men, and the creator of the Zeitgeist Movement, Peter Joseph.

Jami Sherman Triplett drew the wonderful cover to this book. And the best photographer in the world, CS Muncy, took all the photos. You can find all his work at

www.CSMuncyPhotography.com

A Moment Of Clarity Brought
To You By LeeCamp.net

http://youtu.be/bm16wILb_YY

Everything in our lives is owned or materialized or commoditized. Your clothes are brought to you by Levis, life-sustaining water provided to you by Poland Springs, human interaction brought to you by Facebook or Skype, love brought to you by e-Harmony, good times brought to you by Heineken, bad times brought to you by too much Heineken, hardcore sex brought to you by Trojan's New Icy Fire Crotch Cream!, answers to all your problems brought to you by Oprah, laughter brought to you by Tyler Perry's Medea Goes To Fuck A Fiddle! (or whatever the hell it's called), security and/or death provided by Smith & Wesson, mindless entertainment brought to you by the National Football League, panic and fear brought to you by Fox News, war brought to you by Lockheed Martin, Shell, Boeing and Blackwater, the ability to take your 9 to 5 job and turn it into 24-hour slave labor brought to you by Blackberry or iPhone, and finally deep depression brought to you by the sudden realization that nothing in our lives is REAL.

But don't worry. There are pills that can fix that moment of clarity — they're brought to you by Prozac.

And this book is brought to you by **www.LeeCamp.net**.

Let's Teach Children
Real American History

http://youtu.be/qkFhKYJw3wY

I have an idea to help with education in this country. It's a crazy idea, so please buckle some kind of seatbelt. Here it is: What if we taught children American history that actually HAPPENED? Enough of this *"Well, the white man met the natives, and they shared squash. And it was DELICIOUS!"* When kids get lied to, they grow up to be first-rate douche-tards. It's a proven fact. So let's tell them the fucking truth for a change. The settlers slaughtered the natives because the settlers had guns and Satan on their side while the natives only had DREAMCATCHERS! It's not easy to win a war when you're trying to stab someone with a peace pipe! And let's tell the kids that the founding fathers had slaves and Columbus didn't discover jack shit, and Texas was stolen, and mommy didn't really move to Canada for a job, she's in Cleveland fucking the guy who used to mow our lawn. You know, THE TRUTH!

Bullshit does not make for a good foundation on which to build your reality. Have you ever stood on a pile of shit? It's VERY slippery. Not a good foundation for a worldview.

Plus, that dysfunctional, messy history of America — at least it's interesting. How about that for a good reason? For the first time ever, history class would fascinate the fuck outta those kids! They'd be sitting there with eyes the size of dinner plates, going, "Whoa, whoa, whoa — Jefferson was diddling who? Woodrow Wilson was a white supremacist? Lincoln was manic-depressive? Jefferson was

7

nailin' WHO?" That's an exciting history class! Kids would be hiding under the bleachers after school reading the steamy details of Ben Franklin bangin' a whole slew of French inventor groupies who would wait in his stage coach for him after the Renaissance Man Show at the Coliseum.

And kids would walk away with the lesson that the nation was built not by unknowable super heroes but by real men and women — people who were fucked in the head like all of us and lived in fucked-up situations. Then the kids would realize, "Hey, I'm fucked in the head too! Maybe I can do something impressive. Maybe I can land somewhere with 20 million inhabitants and claim I discovered it! I'm gonna make something of myself." It would be motivational.

Wikileaks For President

http://youtu.be/Pjh6tG_yMLg

The moment Wikileaks started I knew it was the most wonderful invention since Oprah created a sexual preference that's neither gay nor straight. All I needed to know about Wikileaks to know I loved it was that it was making rich, powerful assholes SHIT THEMSELVES. My new favorite sport was watching them squirm and bitch and whine and shake and piss themselves and then shit themselves and then wash those trousers, rinse and repeat! It's better than any other sport. Seriously, if you had a choice between watching a tennis match or watching the U.S. Department of Defense go, "We didn't want people to know about that!", which would you choose?

Yet our media acted like the entire story was about the allegations of rape against Julian Assange. Sure, if there's actual evidence, then he should be put on trial. BUT in terms of Wikileaks and the hard cold truth it's putting out there, Assange's rapey vibe doesn't fucking matter. He's just a figurehead. That's like saying the guy who stood in front of the tanks in Tiananmen Square didn't matter at all because he once went down on a panda bear. He gave the world an iconic and courageous image of a brutal regime using force to crush the dreams and freedoms of their people... besides, maybe the panda liked it. You don't know. Pandas don't get much action. There's only three left.

Just Don't Touch My Junk!

http://youtu.be/9jf26rnoeeo

We are a beaten down people. We've been knocked down and kicked and humiliated. We're a shadow of our former selves. We used to be about life, liberty, and the pursuit of happiness! *Live free or die! Give me liberty or give me death!* How did we go from that all the way down to, "When I'm at the airport, just please don't touch my junk!"

You can take away freedom of press, freedom of speech, and spy on my emails — just please don't grab my junk! You can go to war for no reason, take away freedom of religion, and destroy our public schools — but please don't fondle my little dude. You can discriminate against my friends and family, send my uncle to Guantanamo and my cousin to the front lines — BUT for the love of God, don't take a hold of my sack! You can charge me $30 for a fucking carry-on, $20 for a movie, and $5 for a can of soda, BUT I draw the line at inspecting my wiener for radioactive residue.

You can check my credit history to see if I'm worthy of a job at

McDonald's, you can give me an STD test before approving me for the loan I need in order to purchase a frappuccino — BUT please don't grab my shaft like a putting wedge when I'm boarding an airplane at 8 a.m. to see my mother! We'll stand for a hell of a lot, but an involuntary handjob before noon IS SIMPLY OVER THE LINE!

Losing A Game Of Solitaire

http://youtu.be/CKFRFbWfWTA

So a couple years ago it came out that the United States, in all our wisdom, is funding both sides of the war in Afghanistan. BOTH sides. We are paying hundreds of millions to the Taliban so that they will let our trucks through to supply our troops! WHICH MEANS we are paying the Taliban MILLIONS so that we can fight THE TALIBAN. That's right, we are losing a game of SOLITAIRE!

Here's how to explain this more clearly. Do you remember when your crazy uncle, who looked a little like Terry Bradshaw in tight pants, would drink too much at the Christmas party, and then he would get tired of grabbing your 13-year-old sister's ass, so he'd come up to you when you were eight, grab your wrist, and start using your own hand to smack you in the face while continually saying, "Stop hitting yourself, stop hitting yourself, stop hitting yourself?" Do you remember that? Yeah? Well, that's what we're doing in Afghanistan EXCEPT there's no uncle! It's just us punching ourselves repeatedly in the face and occasionally the balls. AND we're paying billions for the privilege to do it. We are playing a game of tic-tac-toe ALONE.

No wonder some scrappy insurgents wearing only rags and sandals are able to compete with the most powerful military in the world — THEY HAVE US ON THEIR SIDE! It's like we're beating ourselves on the ass with a paddle and then suing ourselves for child abuse! We're eating our own legs off and then wondering why no matter how much we eat, we never seem to gain weight.

I think the only answer is to dump more money into it. Just pallets of cash raining down on them. At some point the Taliban will be like, "Please no more money! Just leave! Our kids are choking on dollar bills, our goats are buried alive. No more money!"

And one last thing: I'm starting a campaign to move Joseph Heller's novel *Catch-22* to the nonfiction section of your local library.

An Ode To All The Homophobes

http://youtu.be/yx0w8YkBKvk

There's still a lot people out there who are against gay marriage, violently against it. They run around trying to give gay people self-help books on how to tone down the gay, or cover up the gay, or channel the gay into athletics or community service. And I'm sure that all works like a charm. "Yeah, he used to be gay but now he's a hell of a softball player! Instead of all the gay sex, he's become a world-class Jenga competitor."

A lot of anti-gay feelings out there. So I'll make you a deal. Everyone who wants to be anti-gay and lesbian, you go ahead and do that, BUT we're taking away EVERYTHING from your life that is gay or gay-friendly or gay-like or gay-inspired or bisexual. You're not allowed near it. So that means no more Ellen DeGeneres Show or Oprah or Elton John, Michael Jackson music, Lady Gaga or Madonna. No more Rosie O'Donnell anything or Professional Wrestling!

No more musicals or dancing with the stars, no more guys

night out, college fraternities. No more lifting weights at the gym with the other boys spotting you while you're sweating in a low-cut spandex shirt, no more movies starring Sylvester Stallone, Bruce Willis, The Rock, or that werewolf from the Twilight Movies. And no more adults watching Twilight movies.

No more Serena Williams, WNBA, or parades of any of kind. No more watching college girls make out with each other or dance together or jump up and down in wet tee-shirt contests together. Obviously no more gay weddings but also no more straight weddings. Nothing's gayer than a straight wedding! Come on, you've got men crying and singing "YMCA."

No more field hockey for women or yoga for men. No more celebrating Halloween or getting haircuts. No more slow motion during football games. And no more shaving your balls — I don't care if you have a forest down there and it itches like bestiality with a porcupine. Too bad, you shoulda thought of that when you were hating gays. And finally — no more higher education. Plato came up with that and he was gay.

So there ya go. Don't go near any of that stuff. And if you do, we will not only force you to support gay marriage, we'll force you into a gay marriage. Deal?

We Need A Secondhand Military Draft

http://youtu.be/UPb-3LIA0CY

I'm not the first to mention this, but it's a serious problem that we don't have a draft in this country. Our ridiculous wars are fought by the poor and the bored. Occasionally there's someone fighting purely and 100% because they feel a "call of service," a duty to their country, but that's becoming increasingly rare. I mean, it's getting harder and harder to convince someone of their obligation to fight for the land of Willow fucking Smith and the best-selling book *Stuff on My Cat*.

So, many are fighting out of a need for college tuition, and when you're willing to kill and be killed for college money, it doesn't mean the war is noble. It means college is too fucking expensive. But the end result is that our wars are fought by the poor so the rich and powerful don't have to send their little asshole golden boys off to battle. If Jenna Bush, or Malia Obama, or T-Bone Cameron, or Sammy Two-Toes Biden could be drafted, it would be a different world. We would be a lot slower to go to war. But the draft, at least in the US, is never going to happen. The rich won't allow it.

I think the answer is a different kind of draft. Each American citizen gets the privilege, the god-given right to send one *OTHER* person off to war. Anyone they want. It would be a second-hand draft. You can pick anyone you want under 60 and over 5, as long as they aren't gay. Because Lord only knows what would happen if we had gay people in the military — all hell would break out. They'd be too busy making catty comments about each other's hair to bomb anybody. All it takes is one poorly-timed remark about Jennifer Anniston's cellulite problem and an entire platoon is wiped out!

So yeah, second-hand draft and whoever you pick is not allowed to draft you back. This would solve multiple problems — we'd have enough men and women in the military, it wouldn't only be rich or poor people, black or white people, AND all of our society's assholes would be sent to battle. I mean, you would only get one for the entire war, so you'd have to choose wisely. But still, someone flicks you off in traffic? *Off to the front lines.* Someone sneezes on you in the subway? *Off to Afghanistan.* Someone refuses to go on a date with you? *Send 'em to Iraq.* Ugly people making out on the bus? *Pakistan.* Douchebag police officer? *Front lines.* Someone gives you crabs? *Guantanamo.*

Most importantly, here at home, everyone would be so fucking friendly to each other to avoid the draft. We would all be SO NICE for once! People would give strangers handjobs on the street just to show how neighborly they are. Everyone would do favors all the time:

"Sure, I'll help you move apartments, buddy! What are friends for?! What's your name again?"

"Sure, ma'am, I will definitely look after your pit bull with a thyroid problem and a colostomy bag for the summer. I've got nothing but time!"

It's a brilliant system, if I may say so myself. And Sammy Two-Toes Biden has had it too easy for too long!

American-Made Tear Gas

http://youtu.be/rKV9obvZE4Y

Apparently a lot of the military weaponry being used in the peaceful, sunshiny country of Egypt right now is made with American tax dollars. Good to see my dollars are going to something like concussion grenades instead of gay shit like pallets of food or pussy bottles of water for the thirsty. Fuck the thirsty. I mean, don't *fuck* the thirsty. That would be rude. But FUCK the thirsty!

And apparently the tear gas canisters being fired at the Egyptian people even say "Made in the USA" on them. And you know why that pisses me off? Because NOTHING is made in the USA anymore! Nothing. You can't find a fucking toothpick that was made in America. American flags are made in Guam. Your "America is #1" t-shirt was made in Indonesia. Your apple pie was made in Canada. Heidi Montag in a red, white, and blue bikini might have been photographed in California but those tits were made in India. Fellas, even your daughter was made in Cancun while you were in Pittsburgh. Sorry to break it to you this way.

How dare the Egyptians get the American shit! I want some American shit because we're number one! If there are Made-in-the-USA tear gas canisters out there, I think we should use them on our own people first. Then, if we have some left over, we can ship them overseas. But let's take care of our own, goddamn it! It just makes sense.

18

The Endangered Species
No One Is Talking About

http://youtu.be/rsllHoWT7FY

I think we're worrying about the wrong endangered species. There are endangered species all around us, and we don't try to save them, we don't try to rescue them, we don't put them in a tiny four-foot cages to keep them safe from the slightly lighter misery of being extinct.

Think of all the species that are nearly extinct: like middle-class sweater-dog or the calm, rational right-wing American. There are only, like, 12 of those left. We're almost out of circus-enslaved elephants, and the even-tempered political pundit. The last one of those was spotted two years ago on the Staten Island ferry. Not to mention the intelligent, not-a-failed actress meteorologist, which can be spotted by its lack of amazing tits pressed up against a hot northern front. And although I don't miss them, the red-faced climate-change deniers are almost done with. The last one was seen a week ago on the Glenn Beck Show and was immediately tranquilized and taken to a serene park where it can live out its days among the gargantuanly idiotic and the die-hard creationists. Singer-songwriters are hardly hanging in there. One of the final remaining wild ones was seen six months ago on the Santa Monica pier with three nickels and a quarter in his guitar case. The saddest part was that he was playing "Sweet Caroline" because that's what people wanna hear.

The proud intellectual is nearly extinct and even closer to

eradication is the non-intellectual who respects intellectuals. Also, worldly Americans under the age of 35 are barely hanging in there. If you find one of those, first of all, make a wish because it's like finding a four-leaf clover. Secondly, you have to make sure they're of the true worldly species and not the *"I spent a semester in France when I was 18 only speaking to other American college students and unfortunately I don't remember it very well because I was coked out of my mind the whole time"* species.

I'm just saying, a lot of things are endangered. The World Wildlife Fund needs to get their ass in gear.

Overprotection Of The Cheesecake Brains

http://youtu.be/OIVTAz9nl6Q

There's no more LIFE left in life. Every child is covered in helmets and padding and goggles and vaccines and a sign that says "No peanuts." Every day they stumble off to pre-school looking like they're off to fight the Mongol horde. I'm working on inventing a helmet for toddlers that just releases a steady ooze of Purell hand sanitizer and sunblock, thereby continually dowsing their entire feeble bodies. Kind of a protection goo they would be covered in, you know, a safety jizz. We'd have infomercials running 24/7: "The world is a scary fucking place, between peanut allergies and surprise asteroid storms, trans-fat French fries, and Republicans. You never know what could happen to your little precious shit head. So make sure you cover him or her in Safety Jizz!"

And the helmet would also be like one of those beer helmets — it would have two large canisters of health food shakes made of blended vegetables and NutriGrain bars and ostrich jerky — or whatever healthy people eat — all blended together. And there would be straws coming down from the helmet. But because eating and drinking are fucking dangerous — you might choke, you might drown, you might burp — those straws wouldn't go into the child's mouth. They would be suppository straws, giving junior all the nutrients he needs right up the ol' back door. Much safer that way, and it gives him a little pick-me-up in the morning.

And walking is dangerous too. Seventy billion people die each year while walking is a statistic I either read or made up. So we can't

21

have our little treasures with their soft cheesecake brains just walking straight to their deaths. I would say we put them on permanent Segways, but recently the CEO of Segway drove it off a cliff and died. So instead of walking, the toddlers would be passed around from adult to adult on cafeteria trays. They would just lie there, rolling in their safety jizz and nutrient enemas. And when they want to have fun, we would just stick their heads into giant 3D machines where they could be shown in a life-like fashion what fun looked like back in the 1900's when people used to have fun. Basically the whole thing would be like "The Matrix" but without bad acting.

The Wonders Of Lab-Grown Meat

http://youtu.be/lslk2X7XHVo

Apparently scientists are already capable of growing organs in the lab, which means we're only a few years from being able to have all our meat needs filled by lab-grown beef, pork, and chicken. It would be just like regular meat but without the annoying guilt-inducing face or cuddliness. Kind of like what Fergie from the Black Eyed Peas is as compared to Alicia Keys — you get the lab-grown meat without the confusion of a brain or personality.

Anyway, whenever I talk to people about this they go, "Ugh! I would never eat that shit! That's not natural!" Really? You find lab-grown meat more disgusting that taking a bolt gun to a cow's head, scooping away its intestines and carving up its still warm carcass to be mixed with a million lab-grown chemicals to create your happy meal? You think lab meat is more revolting than slitting Porky Pig's throat, and letting him bleed out, so that we can throw some bacon on the breakfast plate?... Full disclosure: I have once wanted to brutally drain the life from Porky Pig, but it was because I was on a 7-hour flight and the 3-year-old next to me was watching the same 8-minute cartoon on repeat for the entire trip. Turns out 3-year-olds DO fit in the overhead carry-on bins. You just gotta fold 'em properly.

And it's not like you're only getting the *good* parts in most of your burgers. If you're lucky, *if you're lucky*, everything in your Hamburger Helper once belonged to a cow or at least something

23

that *passed itself off* as a cow — like a wildebeest or a giant sloth or a hippo with a hat on.

I mean, you think lab grown meat is more repulsive than whatever industrial byproducts were forced together in some unholy alliance to give birth to cheese doodles?? Or the action figurine leftover chemical paste that was used to create the nougat in your Mars Bar? Not natural? Where exactly does nougat grow? I'd like to go nougat picking sometime on a brisk fall afternoon with friends and family. Just fill my basket with some farm-fresh nougat while the kiddies ride on the tractor. Not natural? What's natural nowadays? Anything?! Water? Look at the label on your bottle of Dasani purified water — it has sodium, magnesium sulfate, and potassium chloride in it. I think I also tasted a hint of nougat.

So the only reason you can say you prefer cow meat over lab-grown meat is if you insist you prefer your beef taco has the slight taste of memories.

Outsourcing Nuclear Meltdowns

http://youtu.be/hipOQIbivlg

I read in *New Scientist Magazine* that several US companies are outsourcing field tests of new nuclear reactors to countries with lower safety standards. That's just a win-win situation right there. Poor countries get a little cash, and we get to freely goof around with some of the most dangerous creations mankind has to offer without worrying that we're going to blast the fanny packs right off a white Minnesotan family with two kids and a dog. I mean, this is a great deal. Worst case scenario — we incinerate a couple of million Nepalese mountain dwellers. Big deal. How much goat cheese or cashmere do we really need?? Okay, I suppose WORST case scenario — our international nuclear reactor employees create a black hole that sucks a billion people into some parallel universe where dinosaurs still wander and the Republicans make sense and David Hasselhoff is Grand Earth King. But what are the odds of that? Five percent, tops? Worth it!

But really, this idea of outsourcing pollution and risk is pretty fucking crazy. Basically we're taking countries that are poor — often due to our own foreign policies — and saying to them, "Here's $1 million. We'll start shipping our cancer into your backyard next week. Here's some military weaponry; now where would you like us to put the chance of nuclear fallout that you so kindly agreed to house? Near the orphanage? Good call. KIDS! They don't know what the fuck's going on! They're not gonna write any letters. Pleasure doin' business with ya. Just don't turn on that thing until we get outta the probable blast radius, then you can go to town. By the way, if you accidentally reduce your continent to a glowing charcoal briquette, we're taking our money back."

Obieber Care

http://youtu.be/sVTPgtBhqnw

Sadly enough, today's Moment Of Clarity is about Justin Bieber. You know him, he's the 12- or 14-year-old laboratory-tested Canadian kid with the first fully-realized CGI head who makes 20-year-old straight men question their sexuality and 35-year-old gay women question their haircut. I didn't want it to be this way. I didn't want to talk about Justin Bieber. Please know that. I didn't want to ever mention Justin Bieber in a sentence unless I had somehow become a rapper and needed a rhyme for the sentence "That girl has a crusty beaver."

But Justin Bieber apparently said that he doesn't want to become a US citizen because our healthcare system is evil. He said his bodyguard (that's right, he needs a bodyguard) had a premature baby, and the guy had to pay for thousands out of his own pocket. However, in Canada they care about a human being and wouldn't send a new father on his way because he's $12.48 short of the 90 grand he owes. "Sorry, sir, we need to ask you to leave. Don't worry, we packed your preemie baby up in some bubble wrap for the trip home."

This shows just how mangled and diseased our system is. I agree more with Justin Bieber than your average American politician on this issue. Even a tweenager whose educational focus has been hip-wiggling and memorizing Usher songs knows that charging poor people out the nose as their baby clings to life is morally disgusting. How fucking pathetic is it that I listen to John Boehner or some douche-head state representative in a three-corner Paul Revere hat, and I'm screaming at my TV screen, "What the FUCK's the matter with you?! Jesus Christ! You might wanna plug your soul back in because it seems to have shut down due to lack of use!" But on the other hand I see a pre-pubescent pop sensation talking about health care, and I think, "He's making some good points. What's he running for? Senator?"

Ain't THAT a kick to the fife and drums.

Ignore The Wisconsin Protests
And Instead LOOK OVER THERE!

http://youtu.be/ouKM1Hvo2-k

So I went onto Facebook yesterday, and I was posting a note saying we need to show solidarity with the protesters in Wisconsin. The governor is destroying unions with one flick of his pen and lest we forget, unions brought us tiny forgettable things like the weekend, the 9-to-5 workday, retirement with dignity, health care, an end to child labor, and 24-hour strip clubs that serve breakfast... I think I made up that last one. That was either unions or Larry Flint. Either way, they brought us everything else, and just getting children out of the work place alone was huge!! Because children are annoying and shitty workers! They don't know how to operate a pneumatic press brake! Just making mistakes constantly, lopping off dudes' arms. "WHAT DO YOU MEAN 'WHOOPSY'?! You've worked here three YEARS! Since you were five! You should have this shit DOWN by now!"

Point being, unions are a crucial part of our society with a noble, brave history. Go read Howard Zinn's *A People's History of the United States* and tell me otherwise. So I was posting about this on Facebook and the Lord-our-Facebook, correctly judging my emotional tone, recommended in the sidebar that I "like" the fanpage for "Angry Birds," the iPad/iPhone video game in which you slingshot woeful, highly confused woodland creatures into piles of lumber and bricks, thereby making them go from baffled birds to angry, or at least frustrated, birds.

And I feel like this is representative of the mindscape of our country and possibly all countries with access to the Internet and/or "Angry Birds." Right when we get involved with saying something that matters, something that could truly make a difference if enough people joined together, we're told to veer over here or look over there, stop thinking about the wrongs being perpetrated around the world and instead think about Guitar Hero or Jersey Shore.

The Egyptian revolution is... LOOK! "Dance Dance Revolution!"

The workers in Wisconsin are losing their right to... LOOK! A homeless guy who can sing!

The Iranian people are standing up against a brutal... LOOK! Someone married to someone from TV is PREGGERS!

So pay attention, people. Focus! This is too important to be distracted right now. We need to stand and unite with the birds, who ARE angry, who ARE furious, who ARE mad as hell and not going to take it anymore because they've been shot into piles of bricks for no clear reason for far too long! No, but seriously, just this once, put politics aside and stand with the workers and the families in Wisconsin over the corporations because next time it will be your family and your job and your child who doesn't know how to operate the pneumatic press brake, if it isn't already. And then you'll find yourself serving breakfast at a 24-hour strip club wondering how you got there.

War Criminals Sell A Shit-Ton Of Books

http://youtu.be/Cmcd6NlQW3o

You know what makes me perhaps the most scared about our country? It's not the joblessness or the innocent men on death row or the children in far off lands making the sweaters our dogs are wearing. None of that. It's the fact that in this greatest of lands, war criminals sell books. It's undeniable. War criminals sell a SHIT TON of books.

Even while the publishing industry is burning down in the toasty digital flames of an e-reader bonfire, war criminals still move units. George Bush, Donald Rumsfeld, Karl Rove, and Dick Cheney. Too many to list. And the more women and kids you've blown up, the longer the line is of people clamoring to see just how ya did it. Nowadays the only books that make the bestseller list are by either someone in the Bush Administration or zombies. No wonder Dick Cheney's book sold so well — he's BOTH.

I've published a couple of books, and I tried a lot of different ways to market them, but I never thought of being a fucking war criminal. I considered flyers to promote the book, posters, aggressive MySpacing — but never genocide, indiscriminate bombing, or torture. Never even occurred to me! I guess that's my problem. A failure of imagination, a failure to think big.

That's what we do with our war criminals — we don't execute them or imprison them. We send them to stand in front of 50 people in folding chairs in a Barnes & Noble in Branson, Missouri so they can tell their lies on a more intimate basis. Which brings up a question:

How do you think Donald Rumsfeld and Dick Cheney are signing the book covers of their adoring fans? I bet Rumsfeld goes with the motivational approach: "Thanks for buying the book. Don't forget — keep your feet on the ground and fuck the brown countries!" Whereas I bet Dicky takes the humorous approach: "Thanks for buying my book. It is packed full of WMD — Writing Most Delicious. Hahaha, keep the dream alive! Love, Dicky."

I suppose it could be worse. These merchants of death could instead release albums after their reign of terror is over. That would be truly horrific — watching Anderson Cooper ask Dick Cheney whether Limp Bizkit was a big influence on him. But I do think Robert Mugabe's techno LP woulda been a big hit.

Point being: don't buy Dick Cheney's book. Wait for the movie, which will star a Vampire and Jerry Stiller and have a trailer that begins "In a world where being a war criminal is a great PR stunt..."

What Do Glenn Beck And Hugh Hefner Have In Common?

http://youtu.be/e_jgE6Hldbk

There's a problem with the talking heads on our televisions and radios. And you're probably thinking, "Lee, what are you if not a talking head?" But I'm speaking of the really big ones. The ones that go out to millions of listeners. The ones with heads the size of small refrigerators. There's a problem. And that problem is that *crazy* is interesting. It makes for good TV, good books, good viral videos. This is why everyone knows all about Glenn Beck and Ann Coulter but your average American hasn't heard of Noam Chomsky. Out of your FUCKING mind is good ratings! Being rational, putting together a logical argument? They went out of style at the same time as poodle skirts and being able to feed an entire family on one salary.

If Randy Quaid and Mel Gibson teamed up, they would have the most popular talk radio show in the world. And they'd tell you about the potbellied aliens that are taking over the government with pheromone warfare, if Glenn Beck didn't get to it first, and people would tune in every week because utterly bizarre is utterly fascinating. Psychotic sells. Think about it, if you see a guy on a street corner calmly speaking about the global economic recession and he's standing next to a guy wearing nothing but a tattoo of an NFL championship team that *never* actually existed and pooping in a Captain Crunch box... Who are you going to watch longer?? Who's going to grab your attention?

33

But the thing we need to remember is that fascinating and good ratings do not equal correct. They don't even *insinuate* correct. Good ratings and correct wouldn't even recognize each other if they were roommates for the past five years. They fucking hate each other. Good ratings and correct are like Hugh Hefner and his girlfriends. They seem like they have something to do with each other from a distance, but you get up close and you realize the girls are subtly making faces like they're engaged to a block of stinky cheese.

So go ahead, watch the psychotics with morbid curiosity like watching a competitive eating competition or a Charlie Sheen sit-com. Watch Bill O'Reilly and Glenn Beck and Dr. Phil and read *The Secret*. You can even enjoy them. But just remember that when the book or show or movie is over, all you're left with is a poop in a cereal box. Do not try to *understand* the poop! Do not *live your life* by the poop!

Psyops At Starbucks

http://youtu.be/1vtWMTyOTUk

I went into Starbucks recently because there was nothing else around, and I said, "I would like a piece of coffee cake." The guy responded, "What do you mean? You mean the crumbleberry coffee cake?" And sure enough, it said right there on the label, "Crumbleberry coffee cake." But I'm a fucking man trying to live my life with some dignity, and I don't say words like "crumbleberry" without a gun or a sick baby pointed at my face. So I stared at him and said, "Yeah, the coffee cake." And he was like, "Which one?" I said, "That one." He said, "Which one?"

And he FUCKING KNEW which one because the other one was called "coffeepalooza" or some shit and was clearly only meant for middle-aged asexual women who wear Christmas sweaters out of season and sit at home watching the entire box set of *Who's The Boss*. He knew what I meant, but he wanted to make me say it because he has a miserable fucking job. He has to sit behind that counter all day getting screamed at by 18-year-old Snooki-look-alikes because he accidentally only put one pump of caramel piss juice into their raspberry macchiato caramel piss latte instead of two pumps. So his only joy in life is forcing 30-year-old men to say words like "crumbleberry" as they slowly place their balls in the tip cup. So I did the mature thing. I told him to go fuckleberry himself, and I left.

But the truth is it's not his fault. It's a corporate decision to infantilize us because they did extensive research and found we're 15% more likely to buy the coffee cake if we subconsciously feel like we're little kids. I'm sure they had a long boardroom debate about whether to name it crumbleberry or cwumblebewwy. They love to subconsciously turn us into kids because kids make stupid decisions like eating 500-calorie cwumblebewwy coffee cake and purchasing Snuggies and wearing crocs while we tell Howie Mandel whether we're "really sure" or only a "little bitty sure" that we wanna open the second suitcase on the video game version of *Deal or No Deal.*

Infantilizing us is useful to our corporate daddies. Don't forget that next time you're changing your order at Coldstone Creamery from "love it" to "gotta have it." Or the next time you're ordering a Subway sandwich from a "sandwich artist" because someone in an office somewhere did testing and found that we serfs are 12% more likely to buy a sandwich from a sandwich artist as opposed to a sandwich technician or sandwich aficionado or sandwich warlord. And I don't even think they're right! I'm more likely to buy from the WARLORD because if you don't, he's gonna spray honey mustard in your eye like some sort of culinary cum shot and then post the video on YouTube — because that's what warlords do. They take away your dignity.

Can Women Save The World?

http://youtu.be/kBYuQ4PsR7g

Where have all the feminists gone? Jesus Christ, ladies, you can't leave it to men to run this country. We'll set the world on fire and then have sex with it even if we're singeing our crotch as we go! We're animals! We're assholes! We're the assholes of animals!

There *used* to be feminists — they were just here a minute ago. Now there are no real feminists and the ones who claim to be are dicks. Sarah Palin says she's a feminist. I didn't know having hair extensions for brains, winking during speeches, and using your child as a prop during campaigns were tenets of feminism. Yeah, you remember back in the 60's when those ladies were burning their bras? They *always* had a confused baby they were swinging around for the cameras.

So many American women are too busy pumping their faces full of chemicals and watching 17 straight episodes of *The Biggest Loser* to take control of anything. I mean, the bar has been set pretty low. Nowadays a woman is considered a feminist if she doesn't use spray-on tanner on her twat. "You won't tan your twat? That's really progressive of you." It's considered feminism if you paid enough attention in high school to spell the word glamorous correctly when you're bedazzling it above your hoo-ha.

The truth is, Feminism was a strong, powerful movement towards peace and love and respect. And somewhere along the line it got hijacked by Britney Spears, Katie Perry, and Posh Spice. The only remaining vestige of feminism is that no man will get up to give his seat to a lady in a subway train.

Women, you have to stand back up — especially since we're not gonna give you a seat anyway. You have to stand back up and take the controls back from us. I mean, just look at the environment for god's sake. Turn off the cooking shows and pay attention! We're sautéing the earth! And YOU are the only ones who can stop us! Maybe the problem is that you're so busy fighting stereotyping that you don't want to admit you care more than us. I don't think many people would disagree that women care more about people, about the world, about the future and about cuddling. Men don't care about things! We only care about FUCKING things and we're fucking this world up... and down. You need to help mother nature pull a good old fashion Lysistrata and end the global sexual assault. And if you do a good job, I don't think anyone would stop you from rewarding yourself by vajazzling Mount Rushmore.

Analyze THIS, You Assholes

Whether we like to admit it or not, we are subtly manipulated all day long through ads and marketing and branding and PR. So I like to do little shit to fuck them back for all the manipulation. For example, the VIP or MVP card or whatever it is they give you at grocery stores and drug stores. Yeah, you get a discount with the card, but now they track every move you make. They run it through some crazy computer system and find out your trends, patterns, neuroticisms, STDs and pet peeves, and they use that shit to fuck with you.

So I'll get the card because I want the discount, but then I'll lose whatever I was gonna save by buying weird stuff just to fuck up their system. I'll buy my regular groceries, and then throw in a giant flashlight, a Hannah Montana cupcake, and some purple nail polish. Then I'll come back the next day, return the flashlight, and replace it with a can of Red Bull and some vaginal cream. Then come back an hour later, return the Red Bull and piss in the cereal aisle. Good luck analyzing THAT, you cocksuckers! Sure, I don't have any time left in my day after this whole procedure, but it's a small price to pay.

And they're probably sitting in some corporate headquarters in Delaware staring at a computer screen, going, "Oh, looks like men over 25 are buying more vaginal cream than they used to. Let's start marketing to that demographic! We'll name it something snazzy and macho like Vaginal Maximus!"

Then a week later I see a national ad starring Zach Efron talking about how much he loves vaginal cream, and that's when I know I've won.

One Day Without Manipulation

http://youtu.be/mCDcB1N9Es0

It's kinda weird to think we're manipulated endlessly every day of our lives. You just walk through a grocery store and you have to go past the impulse buys like candy and magazines and nipple tassels just to get to the stuff you really need. Google tracks your emails so that it can advertise in relation to your conversations. Unfortunately Gmail doesn't understand sarcasm. So you say, "Man, do I fucking LOVE white supremacists!" and on the sidebar you see an advertisement for Target's new line of flame retardant white sheets.

At food courts they pump fake smells into the air that have been scientifically proven to make you want fast food. You ever notice that? You're walking by a fast food place not hungry at all and then you go "Is that fried beef liver lightly drizzled over flapjacks?! I gotta get me some of that!" Even just the word "drizzled" is a manipulation. When you're at a nice restaurant they tell you everything is drizzled or caramelized. You asshole, you mean "poured," it was POURED on, it wasn't drizzled or oozed or spurted or jizzed or ejaculated —

it was fucking poured on the shit. But we're more likely to buy it when it's drizzled. We'll buy anything drizzled. He could say "We have the red snapper with a mucus drizzle fresh out of my face." And we'd go, "Oh yeah, gimme some of that fresh drizzle." All I'm saying is that none of this is an honest transaction. It's a trick. And whether you know the tricks or not, it still affects you. I still want the beef liver when I go through a food court despite being a vegetarian.

So I'll get back to that point in a second. But you know how nice we are to each other in the days following a great tragedy? The days after 9-11 or the Tucson shooting or when Tom Delay was on *Dancing with The Stars*? You know how nice we are? Basically we think to ourselves "It's not right to be greedy or rude or dishonest on a day like this." We cut all of that crap away like a cancer that grows back a few days later. So my question is: During those types of days, during our best days as people, shouldn't the stores and the companies and the advertisements stop manipulating us? Shouldn't they think, "Hey, it's not right to trick someone into the mucus drizzle flapjacks on a day like today."

I'm not even kidding. I feel like we should go into Starbucks on those days and order the crumbleberry coffee cake, and they go, "Oh, no, you don't have to say those stupid names today. Today it's just a coffee cake and at TGI Friday's you're not called a 'guest,' you're called a 'dude eating shit.' And they're not called 'jalapeno poppers,' they're called 'jalapeno fried cheese turds.' And no liquor company is trying to take credit for your brother's love, and when you go to buy a car, they tell you up front that the gas mileage sucks, the cupholders will likely dump hot coffee on your thigh, and you could get an altogether better deal across the street. Oh and by the way, today... the food court just smells like sad. On a day like today, when we're just appreciating our shared humanity, it doesn't seem right to abuse your subconscious animal brain that we so perfectly

42

know how to fuck with."

And you'd go, "Wow, dude. That's really refreshing to hear. I'll have a medium coffee. And he'd go, "Nah, ah — it's still a 'grande' coffee. Sticking with that one."

Evil People Have Plans

http://youtu.be/czq4E2HcrUg

You know the difference between the good and the evil, the caring and the selfish, the Mel Gibson circa *Lethal Weapon* and the Mel Gibson circa *Apocalypto*? The difference is that the bad people have plans! They always have a fucking plan. Good people don't have plans or missions or agendas. They just stumble through life thinking we'll all treat each other right if given the chance. Evil people have dry erase boards and power point presentations and iPad apps to keep track of just how evil is coming along, whether it needs a course correction because this quarter's evil is 3.5% lower than last quarter's. Good people don't have power points. Good people have donuts and Sudoku. It's nothing but donuts and Sudoku.

For example, the billionaire Koch brothers paid millions to purchase the governorship of Wisconsin. They knew that once their governor of choice, Scott Walker, became governor, he would fake a budget crisis and pretend it was greater than ANY BUDGET CRISES IN HISTORY! He would then pass a law that would destroy collective bargaining — the linchpin for strong unions. Hidden in that same law would be a provision that allows the Koch brothers to buy state-owned utilities for almost nothing with no oversight. Both these things would make insane amounts of money for the Koch brothers, and on top of that, without union donations very few Democrats would be able to get elected against the billions in corporate donations going to Republicans. With mostly Republicans winning elections, the Koch Bros would be able to purchase more and more of America. Now, THAT'S what I call a fucking plan!

So that's what the evil people are thinking. During all this time, what are the non-evil people thinking?

"Man, do I like ravioli... especially in a cream sauce." The closest good people get to a plan is "If I work an extra hour at the shop, I can buy two cans of ravioli instead of just the uno!"

Bad people have plans! We don't have plans! I don't have a plan! You don't have a plan! Your plan was "I'm gonna read some political comedy and chuckle while I think." Meanwhile Halliburton's plan was to cause a military coup in the sovereign country of Eritrea — a place neither you nor I even knew existed. But THEY know because they also have maps! They have dry erase boards and FUCKING MAPS! I'm just saying the good people on this planet are never going to get the upper hand until we get some FUCKING OFFICE SUPPLIES UP IN HERE!

The Answer To Police Brutality?

http://youtu.be/p3H4HyBSY_s

I'm in Scotland on one of my stand-up comedy tours, and I saw a news report that the students at Glasgow University had staged a sit-in to protest tuition increases. A couple of things struck me about this, first of all: Apparently the students in the UK... CARE. What the fuck is that?! You're not supposed to care about things. You're supposed to see how high you can build the cheeseburger at the all-you-can-stomach college cafeteria and then use your laptops to make mash-ups of your favorite rap songs and dancing cats. You're not supposed to CARE.

When I was in college the only time I saw a large group of us really care about something was when the local store ran out of Playboy's "Girls of The ACC" issue. But for once we didn't just stand around scratching our asses. We used our collective anger to get that Pakistani store owner deported and his kids sent to an abusive foster home. Power to the people!

But back to Scotland. The news report said that after seven weeks, the police decided to evict the protesters. So they stormed in, dressed in the weird Scottish bright yellow parkas that scream "Don't mess with me, I'm prepared for it to rain!" And they escorted the students out of the building. And here's what's weird — every person involved agreed that the police, who hardly touched the kids, had overreacted with extreme excessive force. Like Thor's hammer smashing down on a mere child, these police had shown up with their endless supply of lethal rain slickers and asked the students to leave! The BBC even had students in their studio to talk about how terribly their egos were bruised.

I'm not JUST making fun of the United Kingdom's media. I'm actually bringing this up to say maybe this is the right way to do things. Maybe we shouldn't have SWAT team cops wearing all black spraying grizzly bear mace in the eyes of every 17-year-old who opposes the World Trade Organization's policies of financial enslavement. Maybe people should be allowed to march outside the Republican National Convention without taking a tear gas canister to the abdomen and being put in jail for three days. Maybe a kid should be able to exercise his freedom of speech and call a cop a cunt without taking a Taser to the taint. Maybe if we put all of our police officers in ridiculous yellow Sponge Bob Square Pants outfits, they might chill out and stop going amphetamine Rambo on a hippy simply because he had the nerve to draw a big sign saying gay people should be allowed to kiss.

We Can't Control The Monsters We Create

http://youtu.be/VGOmOB2we3o

Humankind can't control the things we've created. That's the conclusion we should all be coming to as we watch Japan battle nuclear radiation. We create things and despite the risks, we think we can control them. But we can't. This is a clear trend — we've got Japan, we've got the BP oil spill because we thought we knew how to drill in deep water, we've got global warming from our pollution, we've got Charlie Sheen, we've got the floating trash island in the Pacific the size of Texas. Then there's the chemicals we use in manufacturing which are now causing cancer in our friends and family. "We know how to handle these chemicals!" they told us. ... Clearly, you don't.

And the list keeps going: Rebecca Black and the song "Friday." Humans created music. Then we mass-produced it and com-moditized it and auto-tuned it and flavorized it. We thought we could restrict it to a small area, but just like an oil spill, it sticks to everything.

Even Moammar Gaddafi — we create some bombs, then we give him those bombs, then we have to bomb him to stop him from bombing, which even if successful will create some extremists who will look for a way to bomb us to stop us from bombing them to stop their dictators from bombing them with OUR BOMBS!

We thought we could contain the Snuggie, or as I like to call it, cancer of the blanket. But we couldn't.

And I know what you're thinking, "Lee, you've mentioned cancer and oil spills and nuclear radiation — why haven't you mentioned Glenn Beck?" Well, I'm doing it now. We created that monster. We put him on the radio, then we put him on Headline News and then we put him on Fox News and next, next they're gonna put him on your cereal. And your kids are going to ask you about the caliphate or why we have a gay robot Kenyan President and at that point it's too late! All you can do is put some potassium iodine in their water and pray for the best.

Has The Internet Made Us All Douchebags?

http://youtu.be/TtyJRsdj860

Look, there's a lot about Twitter and Facebook and YouPorn.com that I appreciate. But this fragmentary hidden-in-your-mom's-basement brand of communication is no doubt affecting the way we communicate with each other in real life. For one thing, we're getting meaner because most of what we say is anonymous so who cares if you call the person who made that YouTube video a shit-stained monkey brain? What are they gonna do about it? Sure, they might get upset. Sure, it might force them to sit in a dark corner of their house popping valium and reading *Goodnight Moon* over and over and over and over again just to dull the pain. But who cares! That's *their* life! Maybe the guy who posted that video is a 5-year-old with a terminal illness. Doesn't matter. If that 5-year-old didn't want to get called a twat-face, he shouldn't have posted that clip of his hamster in Bermuda shorts happily eating a piece of popcorn. It was a shit video and the lighting was way off!

I had someone on one of my videos post "Hahahaha! You have a lazy eye!!" First of all, there's the fact that I don't have a lazy eye, but that's beside the point. Even if I did have one, could you imagine anyone debating with you IN PERSON in such a manner? Could you imagine at a Presidential debate — "I strongly disagree with you on the budget crisis, and I'd like to present my rebuttal! ...You sir, have the face of a Platypus with a weak gene pool! Your eyes are crooked, your nose is too small, AND your body odor is not one I find appealing!"

I'm not at all saying we can't be mean. For example, I believe Rush Limbaugh is a corporate whore Humpty Dumpty except without the affable demeanor and less definition in his abs. And if HE fell off a wall and cracked into a million bloated angry pieces, I can't even imagine the king's horses giving a shit.

See, that was mean. And accurate. So I'm not saying we can't be mean; I'm just saying it shouldn't be done anonymously. If you wanna say something, tell your mom to let you out of the basement and let's have a real conversation. Tell that 5-year-old to his FACE that the hamster's Bermuda shorts didn't match its parasol.

Corporations Pay Less In Taxes Than You

http://youtu.be/ASRDb12D-M0

As you may know, the US has a wee bit of a deficit and a wee bit of an unemployment problem, and we're all told we need to tighten our belts. Well, not all of us. Many corporations are seeing all-time record profits. And some of the largest ones, like Bank of America, Verizon, Boeing, GE, and Citigroup paid less than 10 million dollars in taxes.... Oh, I'm sorry, I read that wrong. They paid less than $10 in taxes. Ten DOLLARS. Like the cost of a DVD or something signed by Erik Estrada. Ten dollars!

They're not tightening their belts. They're buying new, better belts made from snakeskins and snow leopard hearts and bald eagle toupés! They're dancing in champagne waterfalls, eating omelets made from Faberge eggs. It is a good time at the top of a corporation. And the Supreme Court has decided corporations have all the rights of human beings. And that they can donate as much as they want to political campaigns, so they don't have to worry about anyone getting elected who cares about regular people.

I know what you're thinking. "Well, if they have the rights of being a US citizen, they probably have the responsibilities too." But no. Not at all. They're pretty much free to get endlessly rich from the society we've all helped create and maintain — all the while fisting the environment, tea-bagging the economy, bending the average worker over a table and plowing them to their heart's content. Occasionally they owe a little fine or something for their raping and pillaging but like with the Exxon Valdez oil spill, it's usually less than

52

they make in a month. ...Oh, sorry, I read that wrong. Less than they make in an afternoon.

And after all that fun they're free to hide their income from taxes in the beautiful Cayman Islands. Bank of America alone has 159 subsidiaries in tax-shelter countries so that Bank of America doesn't have to pay as much taxes as, say, a teacher or a police officer or a farmer. Think about that. Bank of America is paying less to sustain our country than your 7th grade English teacher — Mrs. Pinter — the one who was scared of caterpillars and ate something stinky for lunch every day.

And that's why I recommend you become a corporation. All of the rights of being a citizen, all of the money, few of the taxes, and none of the responsibility. It's like being a highly respected and valued sociopath! Now, I suppose, there might be a few of you buzz-kill losers out there who don't think this is the way it should work. If you're one of those pussies, go to USuncut.org and learn about the actions going on all over America.... You loser.

Is Our Culture Just A Big Pile Of [feces]?

http://youtu.be/qbSF_c9MFlk

Our culture is steadily shrinking and splitting up and fragmenting to the point that it's no longer recognizable as a culture. It's like a pointillism painting except when you back up and look at it from a distance, it just looks like shit. And we're all just standing there going, "Wow, I didn't see it before but yeah, that's a really glorious shit." And then we rush towards it again and press our faces back against the painting so that we don't have to look at the shit for too long. "Hey, if you stand this close to it, you don't even realize it's shit!"

Our music is just a race to figure out what will get lodged in people's heads. Black Eyed Peas recently had a hit with "Boom Boom Pow." Their lyrics were just noises, like a two-year-old babbling to itself in a corner. Something that just gets stuck in people's skulls is not art, it's a brain tumor! That's a fucking brain tumor. Really, what were the last lyrics of a popular song that you thought, "Wow, that really means something. Those lyrics are fucking poetry"? The closest I can come up with is Cee Lo's "Fuck You" because at least he seemed like he meant it.

But beyond music — what art or design or event in the past five years has really impressed you? Even if there has been a moment or two where something beautiful was created, it's been zipped past, ignored, or shrugged off in 30 seconds because that's our attention span. It's like trying to appreciate a museum while traveling through it in a car going 65. And the stuff that gets noticed is the stuff that successfully throws its body in the front of the car and splatters across the hood. Those are the pieces of work that stick with us, at least for a moment.

I think when we look back on this period of our past, our art will be defined by the Antoine Dodson video last year. If you've already forgotten about him, he's the guy who gave an impressively animated yet sincere news report about an attempted rape on his sister. That report was then auto-tuned and remixed by some third party and passed around the world. Antoine Dodson, who was just along for the ride, made a bunch of money by selling cell phone ring tones and other crap. And now, you probably don't remember any of it. You probably didn't know his name when you just read it. So here's our culture in a handy math formula:

Rape + sensationalized news report
  + auto-tune
  + merchandising
  = big pile of shit
  ...that we forget about ten minutes later

What do you think they'll put in the museums representing our current time period?

Does Our Society Only Value Manipulation?

http://youtu.be/GUlVLV-KhdY

"If more money goes to advertising than goes to music or painting or plays or journalism — then we have no choice but to admit the society we've created cares more about manipulation than about art or truth." That's a paraphrasing of something Jaron Lanier said. And I think he's right.

If you wanna make music for people's enjoyment, then you are either living in a van or working a day job as a fucking sandwich artist. BUT if you're making music to be played in clothing stores in order to make petri-dish-faced 16-year-olds feel like rock stars as they try on Hollister's new denim pedophile collection, then you can become quite wealthy. If you do graphic design in order to create a unique new art that you sell yourself, then you likely eat ramen noodles for breakfast, lunch, and dinner. BUT if you do graphic design for a marketing firm or an ad agency Photoshopping the herpes off of Katie Perry's crotch, then you make a good living. If you're working for some multi-national to create the correct artificial smells to be pumped into the air at food courts and fast food restaurants in order to subconsciously manipulate people into buying coma-inducing food they don't want or need, then you likely make enough money to support a family and a river house. BUT if you're producing smells on your own simply for love of the game, simply because smells are your passion and your dream, and you want to create new, unusual, genre-bending stinks as an independent artist in a small studio without access to any equipment other than what God gave ya— then you're either going hungry or you've got one of the few remaining indie smell grants from the government.

Art does not make money. Manipulation makes money. What does that say about us?

Is Wall Street Set Up To Reward Evil?

http://youtu.be/SUq3F5P6FSg

You might have heard of the Yes Men. They do social activism pranks on corporations. For example, last week they announced that General Electric, which uses loopholes to avoid taxes, was going to give back the $3.2 billion in refunds it got from the government. Or another time they told the media Dow Chemical would finally be paying the victims of a massive chemical spill millions of dollars in restitution. Or another time they announced that director Michael Bay would be giving us all two hours of our lives back. So after these hoaxes the corporations have to come out and go "Oh, actually, that good thing you heard about? Yeah, we're totally *not* doing that. Not *at all*."

Now, here's the interesting part. During that half hour when everyone thinks the hoax is true — the company's stock tumbles like crazy! GE lost billions. Dow lost billions. This means we've created a system where companies get massively punished for doing good things for humanity! Our financial market actively rewards being a CUNT. A giant CUNT. Like a radioactive Sean Hannity who's grown to Godzilla proportions. Does that not freak anyone out?! So if a corporation announces its hostile take-over of a 50-year-old locally owned company and firing of all the employees, it's given the financial equivalent of a high five and a reach around. If on the other hand, it announces it will give free AIDS medication to the sick people of Ghana — then Wall Street knocks it unconscious, and draws the word "Queer" on its forehead.

If Wall Street weren't around yet, would you create it to be this way? Would you say "Let's make a financial system wherein companies are rewarded for being piping hot douche holes! And if one of them does something good for mankind, we'll treat that with suspicion. "You announced you're gonna pay the victims of a horrific oil spill? Jesus FUCK! What are you, Sean Penn? You're a multinational — you can't go around CARING about people. Could you imagine if every company did that?? The whole system would break down! People would have food and clean water! There would be fewer wars, death, and hardship! What kind of world would that be?! Not one I want MY trust fund babies to grow up in!!"

Hedge Funds Make More In An Hour Than You'll Make In A Half Century

http://youtu.be/SbxDypHpqH4

The top hedge funds make more in an hour than a middle-class household makes in 45 years. A middle-class *household*. We're not talking about a schizophrenic hobo or a professional mime, which are often hard to tell apart. It would take a half a century for a middle-class family to pull in what a hedge fund manager makes in an hour. What level of obscene does this need to reach before we stop respecting and supporting this system?

And it's not like there aren't repercussions to this runaway Frankenstein Chris-Brown-on-a-bad-day version of capitalism we've created. The economy collapsed once already, no one has a reliable job, the deficit gets worse, our infrastructure is collapsing, and during the time it took you to read this sentence, a hedge fund grabbed up more than you'll make this *year.*

We have created a cancer. And one of the hardest parts of defeating cancer is finding it. But we know where this one is, and as it grows larger we seem to celebrate it. We admire these billionaires as they grow. We think, "Man, if only I could be as cancerous as them. Man, if only I could suck up the resources of this country while others go hungry and homeless and live in tent cities being lorded over by some bearded tent city mayor with a mangy sheep dog and a divining rod like a smelly Moses, THEN I would have the American dream!"

Should it bother us that by obtaining a monstrous version of the American dream, these people effectively destroy the American dream for so many others? Let's have a race for the cure for THIS. Let's all wear ribbons showing we despise this cancer. Let's have school bake sales with little girls going, "Come on, mister, buy a muffin, or don't you care about telling hedge fund managers to go fuck themselves??" Let's cure this any way we can. Have we tried radiation yet?

Ugly People Earn 12% Less In The Workplace

http://youtu.be/-givHHfwo9E

Studies have shown that ugly people earn 12% less in the workplace than attractive people. That's a fact. And I know what you're thinking. You're thinking, "That's the way it should be. Those hippo-faced leprechauns should just thank their lucky stars that we even let them out in the daylight. I mean, God knows what would happen to a child if she stumbled upon one of those hump-backed tarantula-titted halfwits in plain view. It could scar her for LIFE. I shudder at the thought!"

That's what you're thinking. And I have to say shame on you! They do not deserve to be called hippo-faced. Sure, they deserve to earn less because who can stand being around them? Maybe they work just as hard as you. Maybe they're just as well educated as you. But THEY have one oblong nostril and the skin of a psoriasis zombie and what kind of society would we be if we rewarded that?? If they didn't want to blink at odd intervals and live a life heavy on mucus and low on eyebrows, then maybe they shouldn't have chosen the parents they did!

Honestly though, this is yet another sign that our rational brains have *not* won the battle. We're still slaves to the monkey part of our brain that says we should reward beautiful people for good genes. If we accepted that we too often listen to our monkey instincts, maybe we could really make some changes because we'd understand our need for aggression and war, our need to be prejudiced, our need to kill off competing peoples. And THEN we could control it. As it stands we tell ourselves we're purely logical, so we end up justifying indiscriminate bombing, hiring beautiful nitwits, and masturbating on the Metro.... I mean, we've all been there.

Is A Two-Party System Really Democracy?

http://youtu.be/3NWSa6aMoFQ

So the Republicans keep sprinting farther and farther to the right like they're being chased by a naked Perez Hilton, and the Democrats don't want to get left behind. "Wait, we can be repulsively greedy too! We like to bomb things too! We're willing to look the other way while the earth sweats profusely under a blanket of CO_2 and twists and turns and thrashes about uncomfortably like Sarah Palin when asked to name something she's read! Wait for us!"

But not to worry — if you don't want to vote Republican or Democrat, you can always for vote for one of our other grand political parties... like... uh... the Upright Citizens Brigade!... Is that something?... uh, BLUE MAN GROUP! No, no... What about Wu-Tang Clan? Are they running for something?... Girl with the Dragon Tattoo!... I'm just naming books now.

Nope, we have essentially two political parties both acting as indentured servants to corporate America. Sure, the Democrats are the lesser of two evils and as Noam Chomsky says, "That's good because you get less evil." But I think we also have to continue to fight for no evil. Two political parties? We have at least 5 major religions to pick from, 48 types of cereal, and at least 7 phone carriers, But two political parties. We have 6 major brands of condom, 8 brands of sexuality I can think of, 7 deadly sins, at least 3 dimensions, several ways to skin a cat, and I once saw a book that showed 435 sexual positions — and that was without even getting out your pulley system, pommel horse, and Mary Lou Retton. And YET, we have only

TWO FUCKING POLITICAL PARTIES!

And the two we have are so similar that politicians switch back and forth between sides like they're at a swingers' club. Joe Leiberman, Arlen Spector, even Donald Trump. In one party you loudly brag about your love of war and Wall Street and your distaste for gays and immigrants. In the other party you QUIETLY brag about those things.

If we're going to have only two parties, they should be *violently* different. Switching between them should be repulsive. It should feel like switching from being a Stanley Kubrick fan to being a Vin Diesel fan. It should be like switching from sex with women to sex with dead raccoons or with Nancy Grace. You know what I'm saying?

And this won't change until we get campaign finance reform.

What We Should Really Ask Ourselves About The Death Of Osama Bin Laden

http://youtu.be/LaxGfEePu4c

Osama bin Laden is dead. So the question is — where does America turn now? Where do we aim our giant guns, our hordes of money, and our truckfuls of Lady Gagas? Bin Laden defined us in a lot of ways. He was our arch nemesis, our key enemy, our primary adversary. So what do we do now that he's gone? What did He-Man do after Skeletor? What GI Joe do after Cobra Commander? The Thundercats after Mumrah? Altar boys after Father Murphy? The X-Men after Magneto? Batman after Joker? Or Bill O'Reilly after logic? What do you do after your enemy #1 is no more?

We have a choice. We can continue bombing endlessly in places like Afghanistan. We can continue to operate 900 military bases worldwide. We can continue to be the bitter angry man who was beat up on 9/11 and takes it out endlessly on his children. Or we can use Bin Laden's death to conclusively move on. We've finally banged the hot chick who turned us down in high school and dumped Beefaroni in our lap in the middle of the cafeteria, causing us to subconsciously spend the following 20 years making sure nothing that humiliating happened again by behaving like a douche bag to everyone we ever met just in case they had secret Beefaroni plans of their own! So it's finally time to move past it, to stop treating immigrants like shit, to stop sending people to be tortured without any evidence against them, to stop grabbing everyone's balls at the airport!

Let's move on like Mario Lopez did after *Saved By The Bell,* instead of dwelling on it and harping on it like Screech after *Saved By The Bell.* Let's move past our PTSD because otherwise we're gonna grow old and never know a world where people's balls go unmolested. And THAT makes for a pretty uncomfortable episode of the *Thundercats.*

Will Computers Take Over The Earth?

http://youtu.be/Ufkwvktvbml

For decades mankind has joked about the idea of robots taking over. We've had generations of sci-fi movies starring giant tin cans programmed with the love of destruction of Dick Cheney and the gregarious personality of Dick Cheney terrifying the puny humans with their devilish pincers.... which begs the question: If scientists had mastered creating a humanoid robot, what was it about fingers that flummoxed them?? Why stick with the pincers?

Anyway, the idea of robots taking over has always been a bit of a joke but what we failed to realize was that it wasn't going to be a human-like garbage can with the voice of a heavy-smoking Speak-N-Spell and the social skills of an autistic Teddy Ruxpin. Instead it would be computers that make our human thought processes appear quaint. It would be self-driving cars, which Google has already created. It would be automated factories, computer programs that act as your travel agent. Cell phone apps that are better than teachers and websites that are more fun than sex. Sprinkler systems replacing firemen, 24-hour video surveillance replacing the police department, drone aircraft replacing actual combat. Auto-tune replacing singers, an Angry Birds iPad app replacing *actual* unhappy birds, and a loud, shrill, ceaselessly piercing noise replacing Kathy Lee Gifford.

And it's not that these "robots," if you will, are going to take over the planet and force us into endless days of shining their buttons and blowing their knobs. It's that there very soon won't be any jobs left for actual inefficient flesh and bone humans. Once we get to that point, there's only two ways to go with this world — either we split up the food and materials somewhat evenly and all sit back and enjoy this quirk we call life, hardly having to work at all. OR the 10% of humans who control the systems make themselves immensely rich while everyone else runs around in a third-world slum called Earth. But we'll definitely pick that first choice. We would never do that second thing... right? Right??

We Have More People In Jail Than Any Other Country

http://youtu.be/9LTXNAVijMc

One out of every 100 adults is in prison right now in our country, the Land of the Free, and in these tough economic times, it costs states $50 billion per year. Per capita, we have more people in prison than any country in the world, including China. In 1990, one million Americans were in jail. Now it's 2.5 million. If prison population continues to grow at that rate, in 100 years everyone will be in jail — and although I don't hold a degree in political science or sociology — I think that sounds like a bad thing. I mean, everyone in jail? Who's gonna be left to buy Abercisers? No one! The Abercisers will just SIT THERE. There will be empty Snuggies scattered around the cities — like we were all raptured. But we weren't raptured. We're all in prison being rape-tured.

There are obviously some crimes that deserve to land you in the clink like murder, rape, sex with a confused endangered snow leopard, starring in a commercial when you're already a millionaire, or owning a subscription to *Us Weekly*. But a lot of people are in jail for genuine poor choices. You know, some guy while drunk and broke and depressed steals a car. Sent to jail for 10 years. Meanwhile, JP Morgan Chase can steal your fucking car, your house, your plans for the future and get a bonus — a bonus, a face-lift, and soul replacement treatment because the last one has degraded into a tar-like substance.

We cage the drunken car thief up like an animal, but if you accidentally invade the country of Iraq because you did too much blow in college and didn't listen during the class on weighing the pros and cons of spotty intelligence, then you not only don't go to jail, you get a million-dollar book deal and your portrait in the Smithsonian. Sure your portrait will be the one that high school kids take cell phone photos next to with their balls hanging out but still — *portrait in the fucking Smithsonian*. Meanwhile, a high school dropout working as a stock boy at a pharmacy in a shit town where the hot hangout is a TGI Fridays by the highway because they let ya smoke on the patio starts bragging to his friends that he could steal a case of Ritalin, no problem. Then they pester him until he agrees to actually do it, and of course there's a video camera and of course he's caught... THEN he goes to jail for 12 years for theft and drug possession and intent to distribute and an extra year for calling the judge a pussy-faced mama's boy. And the closest he gets to having his own portrait is when his cell mate carves his bust out of bar of soap.

We have a system where weak sorrowful idiots go to jail for years, destroying any hope they had of a regular life while the rich, powerful idiots get rewarded for their poorly executed evil plans with an airport and a boulevard named after them.

How Much Privacy Should We Give Away
In The Name Of Security?

http://youtu.be/DjoCkxGydAk

You can't protect everybody from every danger. Yet we seem willing to give away our privacy to allow for government monitoring of phones, emails, letters, and singing telegrams and we never complain — all in the name of safety. We're fine with the possibility of harm from certain things. Cars kill more people than almost anything. Cigarettes and beer have killed a few people too, if I have that stat right. And fast food shortens the life of our kids or at least ruins their turn on the seesaw and the chin-up bar. And yet we have an understanding that we're okay with those risks, with THAT kind of death. We're willing to take those risks in order to drive a car, drink a beer, or eat a regurgitated chicken-paste-flavored barbecue mesquite nugget ball. So why give away our right to NOT go to third base with a TSA agent whom you JUST met? Because fellas, no means no unless you're a TSA agent and then no means follow us to a room with fewer windows. We're gonna make this best security screening you've ever had.

We deserve privacy. You should be able to talk on the phone with no outside parties listening. You should be able to send that Facebook message of your junk without anyone else downloading it. If you're into erotic puppeteering, then you should be able to watch that YouTube video without an FBI agent giggling to himself in a dark room in Quantico, VA. Whatever a consenting adult does with a consenting puppet of a grumpy macaque monkey is their business and their business ONLY!... as long as the puppet is of age and the love friction created during the tryst doesn't start a fire.

You see, the forefathers had the wisdom to declare that the government did not have the right to stay in people's houses. My bet is that they did this not only because the British always reeked of scones and crumpets and wouldn't stop playing the fife and drums even when "Bonanza" was playing on the 18th century television made from burlap and small pox. I bet they also made that law because they felt the government didn't have the right to watch everything you do. Some of the frontiersmen probably enjoyed an occasional naked frolic around the maypole and didn't want government officials rubbing themselves and licking their lips during it.

My point is you can't protect everybody from everything all the time. Some people are gonna die, some are gonna get broken legs, some are gonna get their nipples caught in a puppet's mouth. We shouldn't give away our privacy to try and stop every one of these things from ever happening. Life doesn't happen behind Plexiglas.

Is A Human Life Worth Nine Million Dollars?

http://youtu.be/7-mEp699_2c

The Environmental Protection Agency says that a human life is worth $9.1 million. Let that sit for a minute. Think about that, and if you're not a sociopath on the level of Donald Rumsfeld or Simon Cowell, chances are it bugs you. Chances are the idea of converting life to dollars is not comfortable. After all, money is just a symbol. It's a symbol of an idea that you could get something in exchange for it. It's not a thing in of itself. It's kind of like The Situation. He's not actually a thing. He's a symbol of an idea of a caricature of a vapid walking tape worm designed to turn liquor and UV rays into piss and cancer. See the difference??

So saying a human being is worth $9 million is not much different from saying a human is worth one million pounds of yogurt or 130 cans of WD40 or 963 Gary Buseys. Plus, don't you think it's what you do with your life that has real worth? Not some algorithm that spits out the amount of pieces of green paper society misses out on once you're accidentally speared through the skull by a drunk pogo stick artist? For example, if you spend your life organizing communities to fight pollution or educating young Africans on how to fight disease, then you're worth a shitload of money to mankind. Whichever aliens have asked to purchase your body in this hypothetical situation will have to pony up big-time because the people of Earth won't want to lose you to another team. But if you do absolutely nothing with you're existence, nothing useful for your fellow humans — for

74

example if you're a hedge fund manager or an ad executive or the personal assistant to a pedophile — then your life is worth, maybe, $1.50.... Perhaps as much as $1.75 if you throw in the pack of gum in your pocket.

The Worst People In The Whole World

http://youtu.be/YfAuwEnxQS0

You know the worst kind of people in this country? Happy people. Happy people fucking suck! What the fuck is going on in your life that you can smile that much? Are you Dora The Explorer? Did you just solve a mystery, motherfucker?? Did you just solve the Da Vinci code?? Jesus Christ, have you looked around? Do you not turn on the TV ever? I see a happy person, I just want to karate chop them in the throat and just yell "Smile now, Mr. Rogers!! Smile now!" The only reason I don't do that is because I'm afraid they would respond, "Well, that's what you felt you needed to do at that particular time. So I'm glad you were able to express yourself in the manner you felt you needed to. That brings me great joy." And that would make smoke come out of my eyeballs.

Seriously though, have you looked around? Have you looked outside? There are nuclear radiation hailstorm tornado-quakes hitting your town and the economy sucks and you're happy?? Seventy-nine percent of the country thinks NASCAR is a THINKING MAN'S SPORT! Seventeen percent of my home state of Virginia thinks that the state flower, the dogwood, is the STATE DOG! And you're happy?! Thirty-one states of the US have laws against having sex with animals, which means in 31 states there was a PLAGUE of people having sex with animals, then getting caught mid-ferret-fuck, and saying, "This may not be pretty, but it's not like there's a law against it." And then someone else went, "Well now we need a fucking law against it!" And you're smiling?! How can you be happy?!

One out of every five people in the world live on less than one dollar per day but European cows — because of farm subsidies — get paid $2.20 per day! COWS get paid more than one-fifth of the world. So stop fucking smiling!

The maximum jail sentence in the US for willful safety violations causing the death of a worker? Six months in jail. The maximum sentence for harassing a wild donkey on federal lands — two years. I'm not kidding! Now stop smiling!

The Food and Drug Administration allows the marketing of anti-depressants to children. They allow aspartame — also known as Equal sweetener — even though it can cause seizures and death. And yet, they required one company to recall all of its eggnog because it didn't list EGG as one of the ingredients. I'm not kidding. My feel is, if you're allergic to eggs and you drink eggnog because you don't see the word "egg" in the ingredients, then you die.... Aren't we all better off? Isn't that the way it should work? Just name it "Darwin's Eggnog" and everyone's happy. I mean, I don't drink eggnog because I'm allergic to nog, but it doesn't say "nog" on the ingredients either.

My point is... STOP SMILING.

What's Real Anymore?

http://youtu.be/QONDb7GVKXE

I don't feel like I even know what's real anymore! Our marketed, image-oriented lives are taking over our real lives. For example about a year ago, the Colonel — as in KFC, as in yum-yum Bok Bok Bok! — snuck into the United Nations and met with the UN assembly leader. I'm not kidding. Google it. Now, this upset me on two levels. One, it says something about the fucking security at the UN that all it takes to get in is to bribe the guards with a bucket of Famous Recipe — they don't even hold out for some mashed potatoes. But two, I didn't even know the Colonel was real. Is he? Was this an imposter?

I don't know where the line is between real and fake. I don't! Can The Hamburgler run for Senator? What if the Geico Gekko became president? Don't tell me it can't happen. The Terminator was governor of California and Yosemite Sam was President for eight years. Don't tell me it can't happen.

The fake advertisement world is invading the real world with the fervor of 10,000 salivating lobbyists introduced to a freshman Congressman. Some alcohol companies now have hot women positioned in bars to act like they LOVE a new kind of liquor. These are fake women flirting in bars — well, they're real women but their purpose and their tits are fake... and probably their hair and eyebrows and nose and tan and personality too. They're living billboards, but you don't know it. You just think they're regular run-of-the-mill tarts, but you're being scammed. Is ANYTHING fucking real anymore?

I'm gonna go live with a goddamn farmer in some slow-as-shit farm town. Not because it will be enjoyable but just because it will be real. It will be painfully real. I'd be thrilled — drinking a big glass of milk that came out of a cow that I can look at and wave to like "Hi cow! Thanks for the fucking milk!" And then I would think to myself, "God damn, this real as SHIT! Sure, it's boring as FUCK, but it's real as SHIT!"

The U.S. Government Is Giving Guns To Your Friendly Neighborhood Drug Cartel

http://youtu.be/bMwaOW59Uhs

Apparently our Department of Alcohol, Tobacco, and Firearms has been helping out with Mexico's bloody drug wars by selling guns to the drug cartels. Those same guns sometimes end up being used to kill people. The program was nicknamed "Fast & Furious" — I'm not kidding — and the ATF allowed the sales so that they could monitor where the guns went and who they killed. Again, I'm not fucking kidding.

This a GRAND idea! The government should start giving us all sorts of shit so they can track it. They should give us mushrooms and meth, hookers and Uzi's, free porn and Samurai swords, anthrax and absinthe! Give us all that shit and then you can watch it all you want. You can call it "Trashed and Curious!" How does that sound?

Really — they named the program "Fast and Furious"? Nothing spells success like naming your plan after a Vin Diesel movie in which the bad guys with the guns always successfully avoid the cops. Did you perhaps get this lame fucking idea *from* a Vin Diesel movie? Or perhaps Vin Diesel himself? Did you go to his cage behind the Universal lot, toss some gummy bears to him and then ask him to use his fecal matter to spell out a plan on the wall? That's the only answer I could picture for this.

Here's an idea: If you NRA members didn't make it so easy to get assault rifles in the first place, you wouldn't have to track them in a crazy scheme. Instead, any time you saw someone with a semi-automatic, you would know "that's a criminal." Easy. But no, you guys need your assault rifles. What the fuck kinda deer are you taking out with an AK47? Are they Soviet-made nuclear deer? Are they Al Qaeda suicidal dynamite deer? Last I checked, all you needed to mangle a deer was a Toyota Camry. You don't need an assault rifle.

And then gun owners respond, "Listen man, when the shit goes down and the government comes to get us, I wanna be able to fight back!" I hate to rain on your heavily-armed parade, but if the government wants you dead, they're not knocking on the front door like Mariska Hargitay in *Law & Order: SVU* with some handcuffs and cup of coffee. They're lightly dusting you with a bio weapon. Your last words won't be "Come and get me, mothafuckers! You can have my guns when you pry 'em from my cold dead hands!" Your last words will be "It's looking cloudy. Think it might rain pretty h— (cough)..."

Climate Change Is NOT Real

http://youtu.be/iUx2rYuhr4o

Tornadoes are tearing apart much of the country. We ended up with more deaths from two storm systems than we normally get from an entire year of storm systems. Record-setting flooding along the Mississippi and other places in the country. New York, where I live, had its coldest winter in 30 years immediately after its hottest summer.

So the question is: When will Republicans stop listening to the oil-industry-funded think tanks that tell us global climate change isn't happening? How long will the GOP play this downright hilarious life-and-death game? I want to see them TRY to keep up this charade. I want to see Republican Congressman and Presidential candidates campaigning from rooftop to rooftop in the flooded Mississippi valley, handing out floaties and snorkels to voters that say "Romney 2012: He'll bring you a flood of tax cuts!" on the side of them. Politicians making the switch from the motorcade to the motor-boat-cade. Pamphlets being airdropped to unreachable portions of the country on why to vote for Herman Cain with instructions on the back on how to hide in a bathtub if an F5 tornado is bearing down on you. Although hiding in a bathtub is also good advice for what to do if Herman Cain is bearing down on you.

I heard a right-wing radio show host two weeks ago talking about how the battle against environmentalists is winnable. He was saying the right wing had almost won the war. I heard this WHILE I was driving in Ohio on a main highway that was six inches above the flood waters. I can't imagine your average Ohio Republican voter is standing up to his waist in his flooded house thinking, "Goddamn straight! We've almost won the war against environmentalists! Time for a celebration!" Talk about out of touch with voters' concerns!! You think they give a shit about whether there's a group of people who think wind and solar power would help the world? No! Their number one concern is finding the front half of their house that rumor-has-it is a mile away on top of a Pizzeria Uno. Their main concern is not defending a billionaire's right to drill for oil in the last remaining polar bear's living room. Their main concern is finding something to weigh down their 2-year-old Corgi so he doesn't shoot off into the twister clouds like the last one did.

Global climate change is happening now. And denial is not just a river in Africa... it's also a river in America. It's the new one where Memphis used to be.

You Are Not Alone

http://youtu.be/PNz069tLU3U

If I had to pick a common theme out of the comments and emails I get concerning "Moment Of Clarity," it's people telling me they're just excited to see that they aren't alone. They're thrilled that someone else cares about this shit. And today's episode is simply to say "You're *truly* not alone." There are protests going on around the world showing that people are done being afraid of corporate warlords. Sure the mainstream media won't cover THIS popular uprising. They're too busy covering the Fox-News-created Klan Bag rallies and the botox being injected into a 7-year-old beauty queen. And if that beauty queen plays her cards right and lacks all intellectual curiosity and gets to the third round of "America's got Talent" when she's 19 and then puts out an album and then puts out a movie and then puts out for a producer and then starts a successful blog, she too can one day be a respected journalist on MSNBC or CNN, as long as she makes sure to avoid any and all journalism training.

The mainstream media can't cover this popular awakening

because YOU realizing you have a voice and can make a difference FUCKING SUCKS for their ratings! Half the ads on news shows are for various pills to numb you to reality, knock you out, stamp out anger, depression, sexual frustration, and regular frustration because those things often make you want to turn off the TV and demand a better world. And a different world is a punch to the dick for Nielsen ratings and therefore drug companies and therefore Wall Street.

I don't know about you, but I'm buying stock in the companies that produce pitch forks, slingshots, and 2x4's, sacks of door knobs, black spray paint, and baseball bats with rusty nails through 'em. I don't know what kind of fucked-up company makes that shit, but I'm getting in on the ground floor. And then Wall Street will be happy because investors can make a boatload of money just before they're run out of town. It's the invisible hand of the free market putting its thumb up its ass.

But honestly, we could force the media to cover this shit. To cover Wisconsin and Ohio. To cover police choking and arresting activists because they're dancing at the Jefferson memorial. To cover the guerrilla drive-in movie we projected on the side of the Koch Brothers Theater in New York.

How do we do it? Step one: Turn off your TV. Step two: Drop your pants. Step three: Take a dump on said TV. It'll be tougher if you have a flatscreen, but you'll be thankful later that you worked out the logistics. Next, get your news elsewhere from now on. Get it from Democracy Now or TheRealNews.com or TruthOut.org or Alternet. You're even better off getting it from a novel like *1984* or *Catch-22*. Hell, get it from the schizophrenic who lives under your stairs and figures out the weather by reading the chaak-ra of his steamed okra. You can even get your news from a Glenn Beck book — just read it backwards and upside down while inhaling varnish fumes.

And how will this make CNN cover the protests? Mainstream

media goes where the MONEY IS. As sure as a heavy-set 19-year-old owns a vintage t-shirt with Yoshi on it. As sure as you hear every missing white girl must've been in the wrong place at the wrong time while every missing black girl must've been hanging out with the wrong type of people. As sure as employees at clothing stores think you look great in that. As sure as every recent college grad better know how to run a deep fryer and a milkshake machine. As sure as that tattoo of that Chinese symbol on your arm is gonna feel a little awkward when China purchases our federal reserve — the mainstream media will go to where the ratings are like an American eight-year-old to his asthma inhaler.

But whether they cover it or not, you are not alone. There are millions of us who can't see a future in the way things are going, who regardless of political affiliation are, first and foremost, anti-corporate ownership of our society, and who are willing to stand up to let it be known.

So the final step to this plan: Talk to people. Don't argue with them about the smaller issues. We can wait until later to sort out whether the ever-dangerous sugary candy should be allowed in the high school vending machines next to the Plan B pills and the extra AK-47 clips. Instead, simply tell people that corporations don't care about men or women or children. They only care about money and money and then if they have time, more money. And like a shirtless hair gel conduit in a "Twilight" movie, corporations are sucking the lifeblood out of us and leaving us with nothing to show for it but a pillaged society and a fiery case of gonorrhea!

And those corporations own our lives and our political system. Tell people this and I'll bet you'll find an impressive number agree with you. And the truth is, the topic will come up anyway because they'll wonder why your television smells like ass, and you'll say, "'The Bachelorette' was just on."

You're not alone.

Are College Students Now Only Taught To Fuck The Little Guy?

http://youtu.be/jcXhQUUZqAw

More liberal arts colleges fold everyday. Only 8% of students get degrees in humanities anymore whereas 22% now get business majors. Corporate for-profit universities are springing up everywhere. Basically, caring about humanity is down and caring about business is up. You can take such thrilling courses as How To Fuck The Little Guy, How To Screw The Little Guy, or How To Get The Little Guy To Look The Other Way While You Screw Him. You'll learn how to put profit before people. How to do a profit-risk analysis in which you'll learn that it's okay to give 10,000 people leukemia as long as the settlement you owe them later is less than the profit you made by putting that nuclear waste under Bubba's Goodtime Swimming Hole! We regret to inform you that the courses on morality and ethics have been discontinued due to lack of interest.

This change is obviously because of a shift in what we value in life. Nowadays it's only money. But it's also due to a change in what we value in OTHER people. It used to be that someone said they were a teacher and people would respond, "Wow, that's wonderful that you give of yourself to help kids learn! You're a better person than I." But now someone says they're a teacher and people go, "Oh... Did you fail out of law school? That's alright — not everyone can do something that matters. Some of us have to read all those romance novels, right?"

And it's not the job that changed. It's our fucking society that has changed. We became greedy assholes. It's one thing to be greedy and only care about money. But it's a whole different level of dickheadery to only value greed in others. Firefighters for example — firefighters used to be viewed as hardworking selfless people who risk their lives to save a child stuck in a towering inferno or a hamster stuck in a storm drain. It was considered a noble thing to do with your life, whether you were doing it to help people or because you liked watching shit burn. And sure, there was a resurgence for firefighter fame after 9/11. They made a brief MC-Hammer-Too-Legit-To-Quit comeback. But now it's faded, and the only time you hear someone mention a firefighter is if they're 27 and bangin' one or they're a 45-year-old frumpy fifth grade teacher with a secret naked fireman calendar hidden in her desk. Other than that, people don't give a shit about the courageous firefighters because that profession doesn't make enough money to be respected. In fact the rich are trying to defund the fire departments because fire departments work pretty damn well, and they're funded by taxpayer dollars... which means they're socialist. — GASP — Quick, picture your happy-place! Hum the national anthem! Chew on dollar bills until the demons go away!!

Perhaps it's time we went back to valuing qualities in people other than money. Perhaps it's time that if your daughter or son is dating a firefighter, you feel more pride than if they're dating a hedge fund maneater.... I mean *manager*.

LEE CAMP

Hey Millennial Generation, Get Out Of The Basement!

http://youtu.be/rJLg4qV_TTg

Those of us 35 and under are still acting like children. And I don't just mean those of us who are sweaty and play with action figures — although that's another problem we should talk about. But right now I'm talking about the fact that we live in a world created by our parents — and not the good parents who fought for peace and threesomes. I'm talking about the dickhead alcoholic parents who sought only war and money and televised golf. They won out in this society, and my generation is not saying, "Here's an idea. Go fuck yourself! We're our own people now, and we're making some new shit! We're putting these building blocks together differently this time!" Our energy is lost in foosball, fantasy football, and Facebook. We take some shitty job that we hate in some boring-as-all-hell office in which we pretend to care about widgets and phone calls about widgets and spreadsheets about widgets and graphs about widgets. And then we get home and thrust our head back into an episode of "30 Rock" or "Tosh.O" because our brain is so fucking filled with widget physics and dynamics and logistics that we feel like we're gonna vomit widgets out of ear canals, which although it might make a good internet video, does not make for a sane life. And at that point in our day we don't wanna think about how things could be different if only we all stood up to our asshole parents' dream of a world based on greed and consumption and praying to a god that will allow for endless greed and consumption.

89

Another world is possible where pot is legalized and golf isn't televised and minimum wage is more than enough to buy a fresh ripe mango on the way home without it depleting your kids college fund and war is viewed as a really fucked-up thing that only happens when you've got absolutely no other option — like having sex while Barbara Walters is on TV in the background. It's very uncomfortable and there must be REALLY REALLY no other choice.... I don't know, maybe the remote is broken or something.

Point is, we have to grow up and move out of this basement. It's dark in here, and getting hotter by the month, and it smells vaguely of broken dreams, misdirected anger, and nacho cheese. Let's find a new place to live. We'll build it our fucking selves.

Let's Take Apathy Out To The Shed And Beat It With A Shovel

http://youtu.be/UCRY0e_euL8

It's time for the extinction of apathy. I say we all take it out to the shed and beat it with a shovel until it's unrecognizable. And it would serve as a message to its friends too — ambivalence, naiveté, and blissful ignorance. They would all know that unless they back the fuck up off us, we're gonna pound their faces in too.

As Howard Zinn said, "You can't be neutral on a moving train." Well, I think we're moving past that into "You can't be standin' there scratching your ass while the country comes crumbling down under the weight of massive corporate greed. You can't be neutral while your mother's pension is stolen and your sister's dreams are repossessed. You can't be blissfully ignorant while your brother is sent to wage war across the world in order to make a foreign country safe for Disney's child laborers." I can't wait for a Disney exec to trot out and go, "Listen, those kids need a quiet environment in which to do their sewing. We had no choice but to dispose of the locals because the kids can't work with all the distractions."

Don't get me wrong. Apathy had a good run. We had some swell times together. Remember grunge? Remember tee-shirts that said, "Do I look like I give a fuck?" Remember coffee mugs that read, "I got up. What more do you want from me?!" Remember happy-go-lucky sitcoms like "Friends?" They all lived in million-dollar New York apartments with whimsical jobs they never had to be at so they just sat around and laughed and laughed and laughed. If they were around today their local coffee shop would have been bought out by Cosi. Monica's restaurant would be an Applebee's. Ross would be a professor at a for-profit college that puts students into debt for the next 40 years. Joey would be acting in commercials for the new pill that combines Zoloft and Cialis to give you a blissfully numb yet undeniably erect penis — "The JUGGERNAUT OF JUNK that's NEVER flaccidly morose, NEVER hanging its head due to the weight of the world!" Chandler would still be unemployed but rather than inexplicably affording a $2000 a month bedroom, he'd have moved back into his Mom's place in Cleveland. And Phoebe would be a hooker.... if she wasn't a hooker in the original. Tough to say.

There's no room for apathy anymore. There are no ambivalence rallies. You can't march around going, "What do we want? We don't know! When do we want it? You tell us!" And Fox News can only channel the right wing's anger into racism for so long. Soon even they'll start to figure it out.

Look, if Bush is allowed to do all-out battle against an emotion with his *War on Terror*, then we're allowed to have a *War on Apathy*. So grab a bucket and a mop. We've got a flood of shit to clean up. And it won't get done if you're playing Farmville.

Top Ten Ways To Punch Corporations In The Balls

http://youtu.be/2bJjEqRQVvk

I think there's too much fucking defeatism going on in our culture. People have resigned themselves to corporate enslavement like it's a Britney Spears song. "Well, it's gonna be around for awhile. Might as well pretend like we like it. Resistance is futile."

As our country continues to be pillaged and screwed with the ease of a well-lubed dildo pumping back and forth like a piston, don't think there's not shit you can do, ways you can at least slow this angry sex-bot down. Each and every one of us must do SOMETHING. Stand up, take a swing, throw an elbow. Even if it's just small things — at least you will have shown up for the fight. Here are some ideas:

1) If your job steals your healthcare coverage, steal their staplers. It's the least you can do. "I can't get the liver transplant I need, but good luck affixing two pieces of paper together, you twatlickers!"

2) Refuse to pay a parking ticket when the state is trying to

make up the money they lost by giving billionaires tax cuts.

3) Streak through a board meeting.

4) Slip a photo of your sack into the PowerPoint presentation!

5) Move that book *How To Be Successful Like A CEO* to the fiction section, move *Brave New World* to the nonfiction section, move Donald Rumsfeld's book to the True Crime section, Donald Trump's to the True Cunt section, Newt Gingrich's to the bathroom, and Obama's to the "he might be a smart guy, but he's betrothed to corporate America" section. Do they have that section yet? They should.

6) Move your money out of the big banks that just foreclosed on your cousin's house.

7) Put your money in a small local bank or an empty milk carton. And if you wanna have the feeling of still having it in a bank, every time you take money out of the milk carton, charge yourself a $1.50 that you flush down the toilet, and then slap your grandmother. You'll feel just like you belong to a big bank.

8) Dump the stock you have in unabashedly evil corporations. "Why I would do that? They're making me money!" Well, if a neighborhood rapist said he needed investors to help him rape but he'd give you 150% return on the money, would you give him the money and cross your fingers that he didn't rape you?

9) If you work for one of those evil corporations, I'm not gonna tell you to quit, but enter some data wrong. You know, just fuck their day by accidentally ordering 100,000 units of cardboard boxes instead of 100. Just fuck up their week a little like they did to you when they charged you $300 to get out of your cell phone contract. Cell phone contracts are offensive! "I'm leaving because you're a shitty phone to be in a relationship with! You're charging me to get out of an abusive relationship?!"

10) If you work for one of the chain franchise restaurants that

have homogenized and sodomized our cultures, just give shit away for free. Tell the manager that table five didn't like their trademark pot-pie-arooni so they demanded a free cheesecake-arooni, or whatever the fuck. Steal the breadsticks, give the silverware to friends as gifts, grab a napkin dispenser and leave it at the local mom & pop restaurant where they could use a free napkin dispenser! You don't owe that corporate behemoth ANYTHING. Why would you? Just because they stopped calling you a waiter and started calling you an "associate" or a "friend of the family" or a "franchise cuddle bunny" or whatever the fuck?! Man, if only the Southern slave owners had known this trick 200 years ago, everything woulda been different. "Hey, we're gonna stop calling you 'slaves' and instead call you 'friends of the plantation' or 'associates.' That will make us one big happy family."

11) Take a vacation with your family along the oil-covered beaches of the Gulf of Mexico. Use the photos as your Christmas cards to remind your friends what's going on there. Send one to the head of BP and write "Happy Chanukah — this oil has lasted even LONGER than eight days. It's a MIRACLE!"

12) And finally go in to a big bank and say you'd like to talk with them about opening a business account. Then WHILE you're talking with them in that little office, slowly start taking a dump in your pants. Don't ever mention it. Just sit there grimacing and letting the smell fill the entire branch. Don't let the conversation end for the next hour and a half. If they wanna shit on the American people, then it's only fair that it comes back at 'em.

Stick a wrench in the gears of corporate ownership of America. Be a splinter in their foot, a thorn in their side, a herpes sore on their lip. Sure that herpes sore might not kill 'em, but one million herpes sores would make them rethink who they're fucking.

No One Is On The Edge Of Glory

http://youtu.be/butYt7YERTs

There's a recent Lady Gaga song in which she sings, "You're on the edge of glory, you're on the edge of glory, you're on the edge of glory." I can't remember what it's called. Anyway, now there's a commercial that goes along with it showing thousands of people, young and old, thinking they're on the edge of glory. Dancing around like idiots in front of their bathroom mirrors. But they're not. They're not on the edge, cusp, or brink of glory. They're lucky if they're on the brink of getting past their Haagen Daz addiction. No one is on the edge of fucking glory. Alright? Sorry to be a Negative Nancy here.

But it's true. There's no glory over the horizon. There might be a sneezing fit. There might be an episode of "Futurama." There might be a sad night of pouring nacho cheese on a bowl of Cheese Itz followed by a ham and cheese hot pocket. But there's no glory. For god's sake, even the 12 people out of billions that get super famous aren't that content and aren't that glorious. Not even Gloria Estefan, Gloria Gaynor or Gloria Steinem are glorious. No one is on the edge of glory, at least not in the sense that we delude ourselves into believing.

We need to readjust our view of glory or we'll never get shit back on track. True glory needs to be viewed as the simple things. It's fighting for what's right on a day to day basis. Making phone calls to a congressman for cleaner air. Bringing your friends attention to an innocent man in jail. Boycotting the company that made the chemicals that made your nephew weird. It's not dancing at an audition for "America's Gone Vacant." I'm not saying you can't do those things — sing and dance and prance and sword-swallow. I'm just saying don't think that you're on the edge of glory because then you ignore the reality in which we live and you vote for tax cuts for billionaires. And eventually you become disillusioned because the glory never came. And then you find yourself on a heavy regimen of Prozac with just a pinch of Abilify staring blankly at the TV with an empty smile on your face quietly petting the birthday card you got from Pfizer.

Who knows? Maybe the day will come 20 years from now when someone I know fights off 100 security guards and shoots an arrow through the heart of an evil North American genocidal zombie warlock, and AT THAT MOMENT I'll go, "Wow, he was literally on the edge of glory." But until then, give the delusion a breather and fight for TODAY.

Executing An Innocent Man
And Other Summertime Games

http://youtu.be/bhlNIR-tdvY

Well folks, it's an exciting time in Georgia right now. Why, you ask? Is it the 29th Annual Greased Piglet Toss? Nope, that's in August. Is it the Monster Truck Chicken Fry Shoot Off?? Nope, September. Then it must be the Shania Twain Grits And Hollerin' Turkey Swallow Wrastlin' Match! Nope, that's on hiatus on account of they gotta clean out the turkey swallows. It's actually an exciting time in Georgia because they're gearing up to execute another man. This execution is super thrilling because it's an innocent man. His name is Troy Davis. He was arrested when he was 20 years old for killing a police officer and has spent nearly 20 years in prison. But you're not stupid, you've seen "Law & Order." All that needs to happen Richard Belzer gets some finger prints off the gun and boom, case closed.

Problem is, in Troy Davis's case, there's no weapon. Well, you just get Ice T to get DNA off the other evidence and BOOM! Case closed.

Problem is, there's *no* physical evidence. Well, you just get a bunch of teary-eyed witnesses to say how horrible it was to watch Troy Davis kill a man.

Problem is, 7 of 9 witnesses have recanted and said they were pressured by police at the time to say Davis did it. On top of that, one of the two remaining witnesses is the man most people believe actually did it, and he was a suspect in the initial case.

Three times Davis has been up for execution and three times the courts have decided to stop it. Now comes round four. And the governor of Georgia, Nathan Deal, is hoping he'll finally get the win. He'll finally get this annoying innocent man out of his fucking hair, and he'll be able to thank the Lord Almighty that "Thou shalt not kill" is just a recommendation, kinda like "Floss every day" or "Beer before liquor never sicker."

Now, you may be thinking, "Well, we gotta stop this state-funded murder. We need to write and email that governor. We need to put up Twitter posts and Facebook notes to save Troy Davis." But no, don't do that because there are more important things you could be doing. You could be playing World of WarCraft or watching "Sports Center," puffy-painting your underwear or betting on who will win this episode of "Jersey Shore: Ghost Hunter Edition." You could be reading up on how January Jones uses spicy food to make her nipples perky, or teaching your bunny rabbit to do a back flip because that viral video won't film itself! You could be doing any one of those things. So forget about Troy Davis because sending an email or Twittering to save a life is inconvenient. And making a phone call to tell a governor to stop a murder is AWK-WARD!

So with any luck you'll forget about Troy Davis in a minute. And we can all pretend this conversation never happened — like the time your grandmother mentioned masturbation at the dinner table. And besides, evidence is for PUSSIES! Who needs evidence of a crime to execute someone? Yeah, it makes it easier, but it's not necessary. It's like opening a bottle of fine wine. Sure, a corkscrew makes it easier. But you can also just smash the bottle on the table and lick the shards.

Update: *Tragically, despite the efforts of thousands of concerned people around the world, Troy Davis was executed during the month of September, 2011. Go to **www.NoDeathPenalty.org** to help make sure these gruesome injustices don't continue.*

Anthony Weiner Should Have Resigned Only If His Knob Killed Innocent Civilians

http://youtu.be/7fXy4SfQB_k

Anthony Weiner has resigned. Now don't misunderstand me: Lying to the press, tweeting your junk — not very cool. But let's put it in perspective.

As a politician, you can destroy foreign peoples with reckless abandon. You can date-rape the environment and then smile for the cameras. You can have an illicit affair with the same corporations that stole America's wealth and sold off the collective good and then stand proudly at the podium accepting an award for doing it. You can stick a cigar in an intern or a missile up a Pakistani wedding ceremony. You can bomb Libya without approval because it doesn't count as a war. Or make laws that reach inside women across the country. You can piss all over working people and fart in the face of the elderly needing health care and still hold your chin up high and get a rest stop named after you in your hometown.

BUT if you post a Tweet of your body, you MUST RESIGN because the American people can no longer trust you to represent them. You have wronged this country in such an egregious manner that you should run away in disgrace. Again, don't get me wrong, Weiner should resign — but not because he's an immoral individual. He should resign because he's a loser. Tweeting your naughty bits is not the way to a woman's heart, Anthony.

On the other hand, being immoral, being unethical — that's

just good business in the American congress. That's their true pornography. Have you approved the bombing of a school somewhere? No? Then you haven't lived. Have you ever helped get a food preservative authorized that studies have shown could cause cancer and gigantism and in some cases, gigantic cancerism? No? That's a TRUE adrenaline rush! Sky diving is for pussies! Wanna be a real thrill seeker? Bring about a military coup in a South American country. What a rush!

Now We Have To Wage War Against GROLAR BEARS??

http://youtu.be/NVzS_WGKizc

Apparently increasing temperatures from global warming is causing polar bears to move south where they're mating with grizzly bears and creating — wait for it — grolar bears. On top of that we're seeing tornadoes the likes of which we've never seen before. We thought Mother Nature was going to fight back subtly. You know, a few degrees warmer, making it harder to go ice skating in New York City in November. But instead Mother Earth is fucking going all out. She's using F5's to hurl grolar bears through our bedroom windows. Nuclear radioactive tsunami quakes taking out whole regions. Maybe, just maybe, we should rethink whether we really wanna go head first at the environment because apparently Gaia doesn't fuck around. There are no preseason games in this match. And it turns out Mother Nature makes the fucking rules. If I were coaching Team Mankind, grolar bears never would've occurred to me as a possibility. It's like showing up to a tennis match and the other guy has a team of wolverines strapped with napalm.

You gotta hand it to nature — she's fucking creative! She's like that Dyson vacuum guy. He spent his fucking life on vacuums when no one even knew they needed fixing. For 25 years his family heard noises from the basement like, "Vrrrrr — Ah fuck! My eye! My eye!" They had to try to eat dinner with that going on. But then one day dad emerges from his cave with a fucking centrifugal force vacuum and everyone calls him a genius. Well, that's Mother Nature emerging from years of relative quiet with F5 grolar bears, volcanoes in Iceland, and a mystery virus killing off all the honey bees. And we're all scratching our asses going, "Didn't even know that was allowed."

So what's Obama doing to help with this shit? Apparently not much. This week Al Gore is coming out with an article in *Rolling Stone* saying Obama hasn't accomplished hardly anything on global warming. Listen, I get it. No one on the right or the left wants to admit Al Gore is correct because he seems so fucking sure of himself, and he's got a huge head. No, like, literally a huge cranium. I met him once. He's a walking caricature. But we'd rather run around like, "Who's he to tell me to change my light bulbs?? He can't even win a presidential campaign! Well, okay, maybe he won one presidential campaign but the Supreme Court still told him to go fuck himself, and it was probably because they didn't wanna change their light bulbs!" Point being, I'd rather tell Al Gore he's right now and get to work on the problem rather than waiting until I'm trying to explain our willful ignorance to a god-forsaken grolar bear who just ate the CO2 bar graph I had set up.

The Gretest Challenje Faceng
The Unitid Stayts

http://youtu.be/Y8YsdROmJ88

When did we just give up on spelling as a nation? I don't think I was at that meeting. Was there a meeting where everyone goes, "You know what? FUUUUUCK this! We don't know whether the word misspelling has two S's or five, and we don't have time to care! We don't have time for spelling and grammar and reading and verifying intelligence before using drone aircrafts to blow the hell out of a wedding ceremony that looked surprisingly like a Taliban death squad from 30,000 feet in the air. What do I look like, a secretary?"

And I'm not saying I spell everything right. Sometimes when I've had a few drinks and the computer screen's blurry when viewed through one bloodshot eye, I'll throw a couple extra R's into the word "slurring." Sure. And the other day I spelled the activity "rappelling" like it had to do with scaring people away rather than what it really has to do with: immense wedgies from 1,000 feet up. (And as you've seen in this book, my grammar is sometimes less than impressive.) But I'm not talking about drunk spelling or words we never use. I'm talking about the decision that 70% of our population has made that any word that even fucking SOUNDS like "your" is spelled Y-O-U-R. "Your dog is driving that car!" Y-O-U-R. "You're going to the swingers party?" Y-O-U-R. "I wonder what swingers parties were like in the days of yore." Y-O-U-R. "What's all over my bed sheets? Urine?" Y-O-U-R-N. And we've fucking obliterated the words "they're" and "definitely." Definitely now has at least nine widely accepted spellings, all of which seem to contain a wayward letter A. And if you look closely at that A, you can see even IT doesn't know what the fuck it's doing there. It looks scared and confused like Elisabeth Hasselbeck on "The View."

And here's my biggest problem with this. This is not the days of YORE when in order to spell a word right you'd have to grab a big ol' dictionary, throw it at your slave in order to get his attention and tell him to ride his horse an hour to the town wordsmith who would consult several scholarly tomes before chiseling the correct spelling into a slab of granite. QUITE THE CONTRARY! There's a little red line under almost every misspelled word we type screaming at us, "This word right here — it's fucked up! I — a computer far smarter than you — am almost certain that the word definitely does not have a silent G and an umlaut."

Are we just THAT full of ourselves as a nation that we think the computer couldn't possibly know this shit better than we do? Or does everyone just think the bright red line is the internet's way of saying, "Great job! I'm going to celebrate your excellent spelling with a flamboyant red boa! Hurrah!"

And it's one thing if you're misspelling words while sexting or tweeting or sometimes the Esquire magazine just doesn't have enough big goofy W's to finish out your ransom note. I can sympathize with that. BUT when people are arguing politics or foreign policy, it kinda affects your fucking argument. Demanding abortion should be illegal should not be done while simultaneously demanding abortion should be spelled with an "s-h". Or maybe you're taking the pro-choice stance of "It's my word, I can decide what's inside of it."

Other countries insist we're ignorant because we don't know other languages. And I can't argue because I can't speak any others

— except of course the language of love, but a lot of good that does you in Yugoslavia. The road signs are almost NEVER translated into love. I'm just saying, if we're not going to speak other languages, perhaps we should at least speak our own!

Without Unions America Would Red, White, And Blow!

http://youtu.be/zhx1CB5LmZI

As many of you know, the Republican Party — a fully-owned subsidiary of Koch Bros. Industries — has decided their number one goal is to knock the knees out from under your average working man by destroying collective bargaining, pensions, health care, and unions in general. Luckily Obama and the Democrats have STOOD UP to this attack with the strength of an arthritic jellyfish!

When I'm arguing with someone about unions, and explaining that we need strong, healthy unions to have a high standard of living in this country, I'm always amazed when the person says, "They slow down companies and make them unable to compete globally. So all the jobs are shipped overseas." But don't you understand what goes on overseas? In China and Indonesia and Bangladesh and other countries that 60% of Americas think are fucking foods? Haven't you heard? It's workers crammed so tight they're sitting on each other's laps working 20-hour shifts. If you lose a hand in the machine, they give you a new job that only requires the other hand. If you lose a hand in a food processing machine, the company doesn't stop the machine; they just announce that one lucky customer will find a wedding ring and a wrist watch in their fucking instant babaganoush.

Bathroom breaks are a privilege awarded to those workers who have been with the factory over three years and lost not more than one appendage or eyeball. There is no maternity leave. There is no daycare — but you don't need daycare because you can watch your toddler yourself, seeing as he's working on the machine next to you. Sexual harassment IS frowned upon except on special harassment days, which are held the first Monday, Tuesday, and Thursday of every week. You are paid ten cents per hour but don't go on a shopping spree just yet. You owe the company five cents per hour to rent the spot where you work and one cent per hour tip for the honor of working there.

Point is it's not a pleasant existence, and YOU — who claim to be pro-American, who wave the red, white, and blue when you so much as take a shit — YOU want America to red, white, and BLOW! You want us to quote-unquote "be competitive" with THAT?? I think you should run as far as possible from that like there's a rabid Kelly Ripa behind you or an Arnold Schwarzenegger who thinks you have the antidote to paternity tests. We should RUN from this version of America you've envisioned in which workers have no rights, cereal boxes have wrist watches inside, Triscuit boxes have wrists inside, and employee lunch rooms are sparkling clean because lunch isn't allowed.

"Being competitive" sounds SO wonderful. But there's another option — being BETTER THAN. And that can be measured in workers' rights. During World War II we could've "been competitive" with Hitler and seen how many Jews we could round up and how much of Canada we could invade and how silly a mustache we could've grown. And some people probably argued that if we weren't competitive with Germany then all the good Jew-catching jobs would move overseas. But luckily, instead, we decided to be BETTER THAN Germany. We created our OWN American Jew-catching jobs... Wait, no, that's not what I meant. But you get my point.

Let's be *better than* the sweatshops overseas rather than trying to become them.

You Can't Spell CORRUPT
Without C-O-U-R-T

http://youtu.be/fHoaF-i6RtA

Today's topic, boys and girls, is called "conflict of interest." And by boys and girls, I mean those of you out there who are Supreme Court Justices. Now, don't be scared by the phrase "conflict of interest." It's big and frightening, but we'll get through this.

"Conflict of interest" is when something in your life has the possibility to corrupt your motivation in another area. For example, if you're a doctor in charge of prescribing medication but you're also given gifts from the drug companies. That's a *conflict of interest*. If you're telling people that the president is part of a cabal of Muslim space aliens set on destroying the value of the dollar and then you also shill for gold coins during the commercial break — Glenn Beck, I'm looking in your direction — then that's a *conflict of interest*. If you give no-bid contracts to a company while you're getting paid by that company, then that's a *conflict of interest*. Dick Cheney can tell you about that, if you'd like to hear more. If you're running for President and you weren't blessed with a cerebral cortex — (cough) Michelle Bachmann (cough) — then that's not technically a conflict of interest. But it kinda sucks for you.

Are you starting to catch on, those of you wearing long black robes right now who aren't members of a cult? If you are a Supreme Court Justice and at the same time you are receiving money and gifts from corporations that have cases appearing before your court — then that's called what? Clarence Thomas, did you raise your hand? No, "cool" is not the right answer! It's NOT COOL! In fact, it's the opposite of cool. In fact, it's a *conflict of interest* on the same level as a lifeguard who's also a shark.

Or a pimp who sells AIDS medication...

or a politician who gets money from for-profit prisons and then makes the laws that put the people in prison...

or a plastic surgeon who gave you your tits and then judges the wet tee-shirt contest you're a finalist in...

or a psychotherapist telling you that you should keep seeing him as long as you have low self esteem and as long as the two of you are dating...

or a graham cracker and chocolate salesman who has a monopoly on marshmallows and matches...

or a police officer who's in the Klan...

or a Supreme Court Justice deciding the 2000 presidential election when he has family members who work on the FUCKING BUSH CAMPAIGN!...

or a Supreme Court justice who has a wife who is one of the top people in the Fox News-created Tea Party and speaks publicly and loudly about issues her husband will ultimately rule on...

or a boa constrictor who works at a doggie daycare.

Point is — Clarence Thomas MUST resign. He's making a mockery of our system that until he showed up had only been a gigantic joke. Now he's turned it into the "Annie Hall" of judicial systems — it's a fucking Oscar-winning comedy. In 1969 Justice Abe Fortas resigned in disgrace after playing the same games. And now it's time for the dishonorable Mr. Thomas to follow suit. Don't worry, I'm sure there are plenty of jobs in the Tea Party. And I heard doggie daycares will hire just about anybody.

Is Our Wildlife On Antidepressants?

http://youtu.be/LqvDJB_aNqc

It's come to light that a lot of our fish swimming around in our waters are filled with antidepressants that have filtered into the rivers and streams. So you see, there are some positives to pollution. Those fish are fucking living it up! Happiest fish in the world. We should extend this policy to more animals. Penguins would stop bitching about losing their habitats if they only had a little ecstasy. Sea turtles wouldn't complain about the oil if they were swimming in both oil and codeine. Snakes probably wouldn't be so bitey if they had a little lithium. Maybe we could pour some scotch whiskey in the water, some LSD. If this planet is gonna go down, let's go down happy.

Advertisements Are Straight-Up Assholes

http://youtu.be/b35RT-pwLRQ

Advertisements are assholes. Really, imagine if ads were real dudes. Just a guy walking up to you and going:

"Hey, hey you! You know you'd really get hot chicks if you wore these jeans and drank this beer. I'm talking HOT chicks — not that ugly girl you call a girlfriend. And if you see her, tell her to lose a little weight and dress a little better — but she can do it with these pills and these boots and this hairspray. But also you should both be eating this kind of ice cream and drinking this soda and smoking these. But your teeth are a little yellow — better use this whitening shit if you want the hot girls to fuck ya. By the way, you're not happy with that penis size are ya? I mean, if you are, that's cool. Some girls are into — what would you call that — fun size? Some girls like fun size. I've never met any, but I'm sure they're out there. But if you change your mind, you just take these pills and within a week you'll need two people to carry your cock for you like the train on a wedding dress....

"But how are you going to call up your cock carriers with that piece of shit phone you have?? You should really buy this phone because it has swipey-touchy-bullshit technology that makes you think people who own it are better than you. And they are. They ARE better than you. Simply by virtue of having that phone. God, all this stuff you need and don't have is making me anxious. Is it making you anxious? Is it? Is it? Is it? Are you anxious now? Are ya? Are ya? Are ya? You should probably tell your doctor to give you

114

these pills. They'll take away all your anxiety — and a pleasant side effect, they also make your cock shiny and manageable with extra bounce. Crap, I gotta go — your girl just decided she looks pretty good in a vintage dress, and I gotta turn that around quick before she decides to stop taking the Prozac-Ambien cocktail and then stops shopping continuously in order to fill the void created by her self hatred created by me."

So, would you hang out with that guy?

Stealing Water From Children
And Other Good Business Practices

http://youtu.be/waLyQh6KTZA

I was eating lunch with a friend and he said to me "Lee, being unethical is bad for business so the large corporations aren't going to do it." I didn't respond immediately because I had to finish pulling a cannoli out of my nasal passage where I had inadvertently snorted it. Being unethical is bad for business?? Apparently my friend was Amish and had never heard of Exxon, Shell, Halliburton, Nike, Adidas, Disney, Boeing, Fidelity, JP Morgan Chase, Pfizer, Bank of America, Nestle, Wal-Mart, Blue Cross Blue Shield, and let's see, has BP done anything wrong? I consider collecting and hiding oil-covered dolphin carcasses by the cover of night a mitzvah. So no, I don't think BP has done anything wrong. But the others are some of the most unethical corporations in the world AND the most successful.

- **Coca-Cola** has had union organizers murdered in South America, but in their defense the union organizers WERE demanding TWO bathroom breaks a day, which let's face it, is a little high maintenance. So execution might have been the lesser of two evils.

- **Nestle**, which owns a large percentage of all bottled water, goes into poor communities, grabs up the water for cheap or free and then sells it back to the people — sometimes at prices they can hardly afford. But then again, that might be the right thing to do because the people in places like Pakistan were heavily over-watered. Rumor has it they had water flowing out of their eyes because they were fat on water. There's nothing that disgusts me more than water obesity! I even heard they had so much water they were BATHING in it — like it grew on trees or something!

• **Disney** REALLY loves children. So much so that they lovingly give them jobs in their factories in China. But you know what they say, "Mo money, mo problems!" So rather than burden those children with the problems of money, they hardly give the kids any. I mean, who can get upset with that??

• **Fidelity** is largely responsible for the funding of genocide in Sudan. But you know what? They have a positive, upbeat attitude about it. I heard they were thinking of changing their motto to "We put the fun back into funding genocide." And they've also been serving a lovely warm apple drink at their headquarters that they're calling "genocider," which is, you know, cute and self-deprecating. I love a corporation that doesn't take itself too seriously.

• A drug manufacturer named **Forest Labs** was marketing the anti-depressant Celexa to children when it wasn't even approved for children. But life's tough for a 7-year-old these days. Sometimes you ask for Pikachu for your birthday and you get Ashachu. And sure you contemplate taking a rusty razor blade to your wrists because who wouldn't?? But luckily there are strong chemicals designed to alter your core emotions and mental activity and Forest Labs is there to give you those pills. Sure, they might not be "safe," and they might not be "fully tested" but "fully tested" is for pussies and "safe" is for queers. Real men get brain tumors by age 17. And when they get those brain tumors, it doesn't bother them because they're pumped full of Celexa to the point that a brain tumor sounds like fun!

Celexa turns brain tumor into brain *humor*!

Of course, my friend COULD argue that Forest Labs got caught and was forced to settle out of court for $300 million, which shows that bad companies get punished. But don't forget that Celexa brought in $2.3 BILLION in one year. So you turn a few kids into vegetables, you pay out 300 mill, and you take in $2 billion. Not a bad year on the free market.

Being unethical is to making money what Viagra is to hard-ons. Most of you already knew this. But after hearing five people tell me being unethical is bad for business, I couldn't resist. And even in the case of **News Corp**, which was recently having immense trouble in Britain after being caught breaking laws, the end result was a couple of rainy days for the Murdoch family. It certainly doesn't seem like News Corp is going to disappear anytime soon.

Racism Doesn't Work Very Well Anymore

I think everyone needs to realize we're almost to the point that racism doesn't work anymore. Not that it ever was correct, but at least there used to be defined peoples. You could say, "That guy is black," and not be wrong. And if you hated black people or white people or whatever you could say, "I hate that black guy" or "I hate that white guy" and be correct. You'd be a complete and crusty asshole, but you would have made a correct statement.

But we're almost to the point that everyone is so racially mixed, racism doesn't work. Racism usually ends up like this now:

Guy #1: Fuck that guy! I hate Mexicans!

Guy #2: He's Philipino!

Guy #1: Well, then I hate Philipinos!

Guy #2: Well, he's only a quarter Philipino, the rest is Russian and German.

Guy #1: Well, then, I hate — that thing. Him, I hate HIM!

It doesn't work anymore. I mean, in order to be a racist you have to have a color key with you and books about various countries, and it takes a lot of research. And I don't think racists have that kind of work ethic.

For Rich People Only

http://youtu.be/1wll9sQPdyQ

This is a special episode of Moment Of Clarity because this one is only for people earning over $1 million a year. The really rich people out there. So if you don't earn that much, just turn it off or look away or go eat icy pops or whatever it is poor people do. Rich guys: Listen up — I know how you can keep being really rich forever more. And I know you're worried about it because you look around and you see poor people getting angry and Wall Street jumping up and down like a nitwit opening the right briefcase on the Howie Mandel briefcase game show. And there's immigrants everywhere you look, and no matter how often you spray for them, they keep coming back. So you're worried about your money. I get it.

And your response has been to grab everything you can from the middle and lower class. You cut health care, cut pensions, cut social security, raise taxes on the poor, increase college tuition, cut unions, cut everything designed for the common good — schools, libraries, transportation, etc. so that you can collect a *little more* money. But here's the thing — you can only cut so much before America no longer exists. And there won't be a middle class to buy all that shit that made you rich. You are not only butchering the goose that lays the golden eggs, you're humping it in the face and then setting fire to its carcass. If you instead let the golden goose live, let the middle class remain, then you could keep milking us for generations to come! I don't know why you're milking a goose, but you get the point.

120

Just give us our stupid shit, our iPads, our video games, our recliners with beer refrigerators in the side, our foam pool noodles. Give us health care and minimum wage and public parks and stable bridges and flood levees and social security. Give us that stuff and I promise you the masses of geese will shut up and stay blind and in line. We'll go shopping every weekend like good sheep and think that kitchen remodeling really fucking matters. We'll buy big-ass cars that are way over-priced and go on vacations to manufactured lands void of meaning but packed full of nonsense and nonevents like Disney Land and Las Vegas, where we'll dump a month's pay into your slot machines and your manufactured dreams. Just STOP DEMOLISHING OUR SOCIETY and we'll faithfully hand you golden eggs. But as it stands, you're milking the shit out of our eggs to the point that our udders are chaffed and tired and tapped out, and soon we sheep-cow-geese things are gonna rise up because you had the nerve to repossess our pool noodles!

Getting Pissed On By The Power Elite

http://youtu.be/ZPV_8gM5pVs

Mushrooms of the genus Amanita possess hallucinogenic effects and have been used by Siberian shamans as a psychotropic drug for centuries. However, these mushrooms are rare and often only the richest in the village can afford them. But the hallucinogenic agent passes unchanged through the urine. So the peasants traditionally have collected the rich man's piss in order to get themselves high.

America is now in a similar position. The top 1% owns the same amount of wealth as the bottom 40%, and we're left standing below their penthouses, getting pissed on, and thanking them for the privilege. If you're in this situation there's three ways you can respond.

1) Refuse the urine — but in our case the trickle is filled with money, so we can't easily refuse it.

2) Drink it angrily while finding ways to fight back, ways to interrupt the mushroom supply chain and make it a more fair system.

3) Drink the trickle happily and convince yourself that it's a great system and you love getting pissed on. If anyone stands up and says there's a better way, you shout them down and call them unpatriotic and perhaps a "queer" for good measure. Just keep taking the piss with a smile on your face and thank the power elite for being so generous as to piss in your general direction!

Right now most of us are choosing that third option. "Thank you, billionaires! As our economy struggles to recover after being pillaged, and most of us fight to make ends meet, you're actually richer than you were before the collapse. BUT every once in awhile your piss splatters a couple nickels our way. And therefore we're going to keep voting for you and your friends. We'll keep using your banks and stores, your media outlets and whorehouses! Just make sure to piss a little on my shoes. Just promise us that you'll give us 20 cents off that blue stuff that goes in the toilet and 40 cents off that piece of plastic that protects our cell phones. And not only will we KEEP propping you up, we'll even do your dirty work for you. We'll attack people who criticize you for pissing on us. We'll tear gas OUR OWN FUCKING KIDS who try to fight against the madness! We'll listen to your propaganda and verbally attack teachers and cops for having the temerity to HAVE health care. We'll even act friendly to the banker who tells us our home has been foreclosed on because we're trying to maintain a sense of decency that you all abandoned long ago. Just please DON'T AVERT YOUR TRICKLE!"

Are Our Schools Crushing Creativity?

http://youtu.be/j36Gog1EP3I

I was listening to a speech by Sir Kenneth Robinson in which he referenced a study done with kindergarteners that showed that 98% of them scored in the genius level on divergent thinking, which is kinda like creativity. They were tested eight years later and hardly any of them scored in the genius range. Basically our schools beat the creativity out of us in an IMPRESSIVELY efficient manner. If a person was tasked with devising a creativity annihilation machine, they could hardly do better than the schools of the United States of America... with Carlos Mencia coming in at a close second.

Our schools do not teach much more than rote memorization and sometimes hard work. If you have a photographic memory then you are a straight A student. Doesn't matter if you're more ethically bankrupt than Dick Cheney, more socially inept than Ted Kaczynski, less creative than Snooki and have less emotional intelligence than Ozzy Osbourne — you could still be the valedictorian.

The closest our schools get to teaching anything about emotion is a Sylvia Plath poem and the gym coach slapping your ass during a basketball game and leaving his hand there a little too long... alright, *a lot* too long. The closest they get to helping you explore your senses is teaching you that if you close your eyes when you bite into the Salisbury steak, it almost tastes like something that came from an animal.

Our schools turn the dumb kids into mindless workers who fear nothing more than breaking from the accepted path and turn the smart kids into corporate drones who fear nothing more than coming in second place and not making as much money as the next guy. If you took those kindergartners who were so good at thinking outside the box, who didn't just see a crayon as something to use to color inside the lines but ALSO as something to stick up their noses, who picked up a rock and pretended it was a magical dragon, who didn't just use pipe cleaners to clean their pipes out but ALSO used them to clean their noses out — if you took those kids and fostered their minds in a different ways, we would almost definitely have a different world. You would have a world with more artists than lawyers, more philosophers than corporate twat-holes, more mad inventors than marketers, and if nothing else, a world with sparkling clean noses.

It's Time For Subliminal Truth

http://youtu.be/z7J2Uit6LNY

Apathy is the new caring. We have so many ways to protect ourselves from having to give a shit. Shove your iPod in your head in order to drown out the thoughts of what's happening in the world! QUICK, hit play on the latest auto-tuned song so you don't have to hear about that stranger's struggle with cancer! Replace hearing about cancer with actual LISTENING to cancer. Auto-tune is cancer of the song!

Maybe instead of subliminal advertising we need subliminal TRUTH. Maybe we can hide the truth inside the popular shit that people like — like Justin Bieber and TV shows with dancers and cupcakes and Hitler. People won't know it but their subconscious will be bombarded with messages like, "Kids in China make your clothes," or "This music is shit," or "ExxonMobil owns your kids," or "You should've kept drawing when you were younger — you were quite good and you really enjoyed it. Why did you give that up? To file paperwork 12 hours a day? Why? So you could afford a marble countertop island in your fucking kitchen? You don't even USE the thing! You SOLD YOUR LIFE FOR THAT COUNTERTOP. YOU SHOULD BE FANTASIZING ABOUT IT AND HUMPING IT WHEN NO ONE'S HOME. YOU SHOULD BE BALLS-DEEP IN THAT MARBLE EVERY DAY AND TWICE ON SUNDAY!! THEN THIS LIFE CHOICE WOULD MAKE SENSE!!"... You know, subtle subliminal messages like that one.

We gotta do something to fight this apathy. People just numb themselves. They cover themselves in a warm blanket of video

126

games, and movies, and sitcoms and cooking shows. I do it too at times. When my head's about to explode, I'll flip on *Deadliest Catch* and watch them catch crabs and then catch crabs and then this season, I don't wanna spoil it for anyone, they caught more crabs than Tila Tequila hangin out in the dressing room of a rugby team. And those crab fishermen aren't talking about politics or how the economy's collapsing. They're just hoping to keep all their fingers while they freeze their nads off waging war against some pissed crustacean so that a rich cunt CEO can pay $80 for a bite of crab sushi down at the rich cunt station.

Some people say we're asleep but we're not. We're carefully anesthetizing ourselves in order to make sure we don't have to look at the reality of it all. But it's time to wake up. Otherwise when you die your family will have your headstone carved out of that stone countertop so you can be with it for eternity because clearly that slab of marble is what really mattered in your life.

Television Will Be The End Of Us

http://youtu.be/ol7pj_AJt38

Today's topic is admittedly a cliché subject but A) hopefully I'll shed some new light on and add new dirtier words to said topic, and B) sometimes thoughts are said over and over because they're good fucking ideas.

For example, don't piss on an electric fence. Or DO cheat off the Asian's kids' paper during the math exam, cheat off the Indian kid's paper during the technology quiz, and ride on the Samoan kid's back during the Phys Ed testing. So today's theme is: We're watching too much television. It used to be a problem with children but now it's fucking everyone everywhere downloading idiocy 2-6 hours per day. Liquefying and zombifying, hypnotizing and then glorifying brands and corporations, products and material possessions. Brain scans show that the brain waves created while watching extended amounts of television are closer to a hypnotic state than they are to conscious thought. And yet we all want to believe that we're smart enough to decide whether we REALLY need the products being advertised, but then you find yourself opening the box to your brand new Doggie Stairs wondering what the fuck happened to your life. I thought every flight of stairs must lead somewhere. But it turns out doggie stairs lead NOWHERE.

And of course it's not only products sold to us when we're in this trance-like state. It's political views and propaganda news. It's Michelle Bachmann and Pat Buchanan. It's death and destruction and drama and fear. TV shows about peace and friendship don't exactly fucking sell well. There's a reason there's professional wrestling but no professional cuddling. Even porn has turned into nothing but angry hate fucking! When was the last time you saw a porn between two people who even pretended to like each other? Kissing on a porn set is about as welcome as the family members of the porn stars. Remember the good ol' days when porn had romantic music playing, and no one was crying and the guy would help the lady secure her strap-on like a gentleman? Such innocent times.

And look, fear and anger have their place. Being angry at the right things and afraid of the right things is good for you. But when Glenn Beck tells America to shit themselves every time someone says the words "social justice," and Wolf Blitzer tells you to be afraid because a squirrelly-eyed Arab was arrested on a plane after strapping a Glock to his cock (which is a very different kind of strap-on), it doesn't do anything but make us scared docile creatures willing to duct tape Saran Wrap around our kids' faces. Television is one of the most important ways that the unwashed masses are made into malleable, manipulatable mush. So TURN YOUR TV OFF. Don't spend much time watching internet videos (except for Moment Of Clarity). And turn off public TVs that are used to calm and stupefy the people. You know, the ones in airports and doctors offices and the backs of cabs and grocery stores, bars, and diners. TV is a low level drug, and it's fucked-up to have it shoved down your throat to anesthetize you when you show up to an airport.

"Yeah, I'm pissed off my plane is seven hours late and stop trying to JAM 'Everybody Loves Raymond' into my eyeballs to decrease that anger!"

How do you turn those public TVs off? Well, rocks work pretty well. But I personally own a tiny keychain remote that has one button. That button turns off 99% of televisions. It's called TV-B-Gone, and it cost me $15 to buy online. I'm working on a similar remote that would shut off Republicans.

YOU TOO Can Get In On For-Profit Tragedy!

http://youtu.be/7Y4OW9t8SJY

Here's a novel statement. Here's something that's gonna blow your mind even more than when you heard Ricky Martin is gay. ...There are certain aspects to life, areas of our existence that should NOT be allowed to be "FOR PROFIT."

> *GASP! Crash! A woman screams in the distance. A baby cries. Did he just say what I think he did?! Hide the kids and get the guns!!*

Yeah, profit should not affect certain areas of our existence. Whether a patient should get a life-saving medical procedure should not be decided by someone who's fearing for her job at a health insurance company, someone who knows that if she authorizes the chemotherapy, it hurts the company's bottom line and it completely fucks her chances of getting promoted. You know, someone who will instead tell the cancer patient to try positive thinking, or perhaps to look into one of those stress reliever balls, the ones you squeeze in your hand. So ultimately cancer lady dies with a squeaky toy in her hand, but insurance lady moves up the ladder where she can tell more and more people they don't qualify for their procedure because they didn't disclose the acne they had when they were 12.

Profit should also not be involved in prisons and the caging of human beings, war and the blowing up of human beings, and most importantly, strippers.... I think strippers should be free. Okay, maybe that last one is a stretch, but one can wish, right?

Profiting from the destruction of lives whether it's bombs or metal bars is REPULSIVE. When someone tells you they're a higher-up in the military industrial complex, or the prison industrial complex, or the kidney transplant denying industrial complex, you should look at them with pity and sadness like they just told you they steal televisions for a living or they write the monologue for the George Lopez show. You should offer to help them find legitimate work selling ice cream or painting fences or spraying the tanner on Mitt Romney's face, or spraying the "little touch of gray" on Mitt Romney's head.

People love to say "War is ugly" as a cop-out when they don't want to argue with you about the moral implications or they say "No one likes war." But that's not completely true. Some people make immense amounts of money from war. The heads of Boeing or KBR or Exxon or Otto's Opium Emporium have likely built Scrooge McDuck-style gold coin swimming pools from the money made from war. Same goes for putting people in prison; same goes for telling someone who needs a pacemaker that they should try jumping jacks instead. People are getting rich off the greatest tragedies of our society. And the free market ass-face killas would have you believe this is appropriate because then companies will build the best prisons and the best bombs. And that's why unfettered capitalism rocks out with its cock out. And they will — they will build the best prisons and bombs. And they'll want to use them... a lot! Like A LOT! Like ALL THE FUCKING TIME! On as many people as possible. Because the "free" market is "free" from moral qualms. It's "free" from having to give a flying shit about whether donating heavily to a politician who will push through draconian drug laws in order to fill up those for-profit prisons is a BAD thing to do.

Point is, don't ever think someone else is going to stand up to stop a war. The power elite want as many wars as they can get their hands on because they added a gold coin hot tub next to the swimming pool. And those are the guys deciding OTHER people should be locked up in prison? "To Catch A Predator" should go after THOSE assholes. A predator preys on others. These people are preying on our friends and family. They're denying medical treatment to make a buck, locking people up to make a buck, blowing people up to make a FUCKING BUCK. Catch THOSE predators on live TV and enjoy the ratings bonanza! The only problem is that Chris Hansen would have to film one episode every seven seconds because that kind of predator is countless. Pedophiles are small potatoes. You tell me, which is morally worse? A man who tries to get with a 15-year-old girl or a man who sees dollars signs in his eyes as he denies the treatment of a 4-year-old girl with leukemia? Now, you may still believe the pedophile is more morally revolting, BUT all I'm saying is it's a close call. It's a REALLY fucking close call. And one of those two guys is doing something LEGAL.

What If We Thought About Thinking?

http://youtu.be/bNvSuilWm34

You know how we're going to win this war — the one between the common people and the power elite? You know how? We're gonna think. We're gonna start spending a lot of time thinking, if you don't already. I spend a lot of time fucking thinking. Sure, some of it ends in "I wonder if I put peanut butter on a kiwi, would that taste good?" And sure, some people think and come up with god-awful answers. Michael Savage and Michelle Bachmann do a lot of thinking, and it doesn't end well. The information goes in one side and then gets processed and mangled, molested, bent, and blended, and then comes out of their mouths looking like what comes out the business end of a Clydesdale... mixed with silly putty.

So *some people* should stop thinking, but in general, the more people thinking, the better. Think about how we can solve this cultural cataclysm; think about whether you're doing what you want in your life; think about what really matters in this world. Is it possessions? Is it love? Is it the 10 hours of bonus footage on the Harry Potter Blu-Ray? Is it beauty? Is it helping others? Is it shaving your pubes into a snazzy pattern like the aliens do with our corn? Maybe. Aliens seem to think it is. But you gotta spend some time figuring this shit out for yourself. I personally think life is about love, art, and justice. Although I'll admit the original version was love, art, justice, and double-chocolate tiramisu. But the only way we can figure this shit out is by thinking and not filling our heads 24/7 with HDTV, MP3s, and POV porn. There's a lot of us out there.

And if we were all *really* thinking, we would *really* have solutions and we would care about what *really* matters.

But don't take my word for it. Ponder it for awhile and then decide for yourself. Just don't get involved in any unexplained crotch circles.

Are Light Bulbs REALLY The Most Pressing Issue In The Country?

http://youtu.be/GXDW1Cty7gk

Congress spent last week debating light bulbs. Let me repeat that: Congress spent last week debating LIGHT BULBS. They have time to debate light bulbs because luckily nothing else important is going on in the world right now. We are not involved in any meaningless wars overseas; we're not bombing any African countries without the nation's consent; we're not dealing with crippling debt and half the nation's home-owners under water — both figuratively and actually, both foreclosures and floodwaters. And Congress can't even *agree* on light bulbs! The Democrats say special light bulbs are our only hope, our Obi-Wan Kenobi of lighting. Republicans say "Go fuck yourself and your light bulbs! And not only that, but we want to pass a bill saying any American has the RIGHT to go fuck themselves and their light bulbs at ANY time!"

Whether changing light bulbs would genuinely help us or it's just a maneuver to make some company billions of those hard-to-get light bulb dollars, I just wish they would shut the fuck up and move on to move pressing matters. A lot of good special light bulbs will do us when we don't have any energy to power them. A lot of good special light bulbs will do us when Iran finally gets that nuclear missile she's been asking for Ramadan ever since she was a toddler. A lot of good special light bulbs will do us when China decides to stop shipping light bulbs to the US, leaving us in the dark, leaving us unenlightened, leaving us a third pun I can't think of right now! A lot of good special light bulbs will do us when much of the US is homeless and living in tent cities. Light bulbs don't run on warm Natty Ice. If they did, our hobos and college kids would be leading an energy revolution! If these were true energy-saving light bulbs, then they would save us the energy of having to debate this on the floor of the FUCKING Senate!

And Congress, how is it you can't agree on fucking light bulbs?!? If you can't agree on light bulbs then what chance do we have on issues like war and the economy and whether Barry Bonds' head is bigger than it used to be. This week our government is debating lighting, next week it's ceiling fans, then ovens and by the end of 2011, they should be done with household fixtures altogether!

A New And Exciting Reason
You Shouldn't Be Racist

http://youtu.be/J1_8XYg0Kv8

Racism is insane. Not *just* because it's wrong and horrible and rarely funny, but rather because we're all a virus on this planet. We're eating away at it until it gets up the nerve to do away with us. If you think I'm wrong, watch that pale guy's speech in "The Matrix." He pretty much said it all. So since each one of us is a virus, isn't it fucking ridiculous to dislike a certain kind of the virus or to say that some of the virus can't get married to other parts of the virus? Or that some of the virus shouldn't live in certain neighborhoods? It doesn't really make sense when you think of it in those terms.

"Some of my jewelry is missing and I'm almost certain it was our housekeeper because she's a different kind of virus. Her kind thinks it's acceptable to do things like that. Our kind of virus would never do that. We only steal from people by using imaginary numbers and leveraging derivatives. The darker virus disgusts me!" Or *"No daughter of mine is bringing home a yellow virus. I won't hear of it."*

What I'm saying is since we're all viruses anyway, can't we all just get along? Let's work together to suck this planet dry.

Health Insurance Companies Using Psychological Trickery — What Are The Odds?!

http://youtu.be/ENb0OZkg8fE

I had to call my insurance company about something yesterday because — get this — they had charged me for something I shouldn't be charged for. It was the damnedest thing! But anyway, during this conversation the woman who I can only assume eats live bunny rabbits, began saying, "Lee, this is not a disputable charge." Lee? You're gonna call me "Lee" like I'm your bestie or nephew or your neighbor who owns two cats but no kids so whenever you run into him on the street you say "How are the kids?" referring to the cats and the two of you laugh and laugh and laugh?! Are you fucking serious? I only let two people call me Lee — my mother and the guy who does my Brazilian.... And by "my Brazilian" I mean my 18-year-old Brazilian daughter. That's it! Those are the only people! No exceptions. So you can call me by my official name — Sir Lord Dr. Camp, Earl of Essex, Esquire. I didn't spend 15 months in medical school and two years at a Renaissance Fair to be called "Lee."

But the truth is it's not just disrespectful — it's a psychological strategy about how to get you, the patient, to give up and stop arguing as quickly as possible. They've brought in professionals and know all the tricks. And one of the tricks is to call you by your first name because then you stop feeling like an adult. You start feeling like a little kid, a little kid who is being yelled at by their douchebag parent who won't give them health coverage. They're using psychological tricks to ensure the two of you don't have an honest discussion. Instead it's all set up like a game. And not a fun kinda game like "Haha, I sunk your battle ship." But a sad kinda game like "Haha, we're not gonna cover your lung transplant. So breathe shallow, mother fucker. Breathe shallow!" It's more like that game "Sorry" where you yell "Sorry!" just before you destroy someone's chances of winning. And in this case "chances of winning" means "chances of surviving." Or maybe dealing with an insurance company is like the game Twister because you think it's all going well and then you realize they have a vice grip on your ball sack like a python who thinks he's caught a balding mouse! And you can't even figure out whose hand it is that doing the squeezing.

Give me an honest discussion about exactly how you're a dickwad. That's all I ask.

The Truth About The Riots In London And Chile

http://youtu.be/QiKWrcCqPYU

The London riots showed that young people CAN stand up, CAN fight back, CAN stand strong in the face of overwhelming force, and *cannot* turn down a free pair of Nike basketball shoes. Materialism is so deeply entrenched in our bones now that the youth, who I believe at the heart of it were rioting out of desperation, out of a belief that there is no future for them or their children, cannot turn down the opportunity for a television inexplicably sitting out for anyone to take just inside the smashed window of a electronics store.

And bear in mind that the media hardly covers anything until it's set on fire or it hits the wealthy and the suburbs. Thousands of young people are protesting in Chile for better affordable education, and have been for months. Yet how much news coverage has it gotten outside of the country? We're more likely to know how many broken legs there've been on the set of Spider Man the Musical due to extreme musicality than on the streets of Chile due to police brutality!

Furthermore, let's not forget that when poor young people act the way they did in London — stealing and destroying businesses — we rightly arrest them and call them criminals. However, when millionaires pillage the global economic system, set fire to the homes of millions of Americans by means of foreclosure, and cover their faces with shell companies, we hold them up as titans of industry, deify them and tell our children to be like them. We name colleges after them and erect bronze statues of them. And once a month some poor minimum wage employee has to polish the ass crack of that statue and that moment is when the billionaire knows he's won. I'm not saying the looters aren't criminals but I AM saying that most of the people who own our society ARE.

Do Countries Matter Anymore?

http://youtu.be/zlxEhw4PEjk

Thinking in terms of right and left or this country and that country is an antiquated view of things — like deciding who's going to win a professional wrestling match by who's more in shape. When I was ten I was floored when Hulk Hogan beat Andre The Giant because I had inside information that Andre had been working on his quads. Nowadays I'm not as naïve. Similarly I think most of us now know that national borders are only a small part of the equation. For the most part the future of this world is decided by multinational corporations and the billionaires who run them.

Sure, there are smaller issues that the leaders have control over. President Bush boldly created a no-call list securing his legacy as the President who saved the sanctity of family dinnertime — even if his economic policies made it so that families no longer *had* dinner. President Obama put a regulation on Wall Street making it so that when banks partake in predatory lending, it's now strongly frowned upon for them to do a corresponding celebratory dance. But in general the bigger decisions are being made by monster capitalists deciding whether there's profit to be made in giving water to Somalia or education to Georgia or internet to Pakistan or the truth to the lower class. Andre the Giant didn't win that day because he was big and scary and French and children don't want to buy big, scary French action figurines. So the people with the money said "Hulk Hogan wins," and all of Andre's quadricep training was for naught. Right and left don't really matter on the big stuff. Nations don't really matter. Just ask all-American company Halliburton. You can reach them at their offices in Dubai.

In A Blind World,
The One-Eyed Man Is King

http://youtu.be/nUTJ6AbastE

This world needs a seeing eye dog because we're turning a blind eye to everything that matters. Why do we have a blind eye? Because we've been living an eye-for-an-eye for far too long. Tit for tat. This for that. Tits and ass is all we watch on TV. We won't stand for flat-chested news anchors on our full-color high-def flat screen. The world is small and flat now but we turn a deaf ear and claim we don't see color anymore, but we don't see people of OTHER colors anymore because the whole world's gone blind in this race to be the race that wins the game. But who makes the rules in this game to destroy the human race? The rulers? Bullshit. They're just trying to cheat as much as possible before we notice it. And we can't make this shit right in hindsight. But there's still time. If we're not gonna fight now, right now, then when? Then? How? The race will be over by then. Open your fucking eyes. This is no game. They say it's all fun and games until someone loses an eye. ...but then it's still fun because due to their lack of depth perception, you win all the games.

The Best Analogy For Religion

http://youtu.be/dMlGPPcJWtM

I honestly am not going to tear apart religion. I will not tell you you should not believe in God or Allah or JK Rowling or whoever your god may be. However, I will say that I view *being* very religious as having a cock piercing. Some people like it. They like the way it makes them feel. They feel it makes them more whole as a person and that it adds something to their life, makes them special. Maybe they feel it brings them good luck. And they usually end up having a great relationship with someone else who enjoys a nice genital piercing now and again. And I'm fine with ALL of that. I'm not going to tell anyone to take their cock ring out. And the only time I did was *one time* when I happened to be painting a penis and needed it to appear pristine.

My problem is when people start waving their cock ring in your face and yelling, "Why don't you have one?! It's the proper way to live!! It's the way we are supposed to exist!! Let me tell you all about mine! Let me show you how it changed me and how it made me better! I think cock rings should be mentioned in our laws and in our governmental proceedings. I live my LIFE by this book that was written by an ancient cock ring nearly 2,000 year ago! I think people without adorned dicks should be ridiculed and told they're bad people. Let's talk about mine for a little longer. LOOK AT IT! LOOOOOOK AT IT!!!!"

NO! Keep that shit to yourself! Put your religion back in your fucking pants! Relate to me as a human being and don't even bring up your dick or the necklace it's wearing. How does that sound?

What Do Peanuts Have To Do With Terrorism?

http://youtu.be/HLrf6m0zQCc

Twice as many Americans die from peanut allergies every year than from terrorism. And yet we spend mind-blowing amounts of money to be protected from terrorism; we give up our rights to be protected from terrorism; we go to war to be protected from terrorism. I think you can see where I'm going with this. It only makes sense to work equally hard to protect Americans from PEANUTS! We need a peanut alert chart. We need National Guardsmen at 7-11s, standing in front of the snack aisle with semi-automatics. We need full body scans to see if any sociopaths have peanuts strapped to their penis, maybe cavity searches to see if there's any peanut residue. Let's send Navy Seals into the Planter's compound in the middle of the night to shoot Mr. Peanut through the face and drop his brittle peanut body into the ocean. (Get it? Brittle peanut body? Pay attention!)

If bags of peanuts are left unattended, send in a bomb squad to blow that shit to pieces. And since peanuts have killed Americans, you gotta assume all peanut farmers are trying to kill Americans. And since 50% of all of our peanuts are grown in Alabama, you gotta figure everyone in Alabama hates Americans and prays that some unholy peanut god will wipe us all out. So let me be the first to say, "Fuck you, Alabama! You fucking un-American peanut terrorists! And that goes for you too Ali Velshi on CNN because you kinda look like a peanut so I'll see you in Guantanamo, bitch!"

And we can't possibly let these peanut assholes fly on a plane. They're twice as dangerous as regular terrorists! And that goes double for anyone wearing a top hat and a monocle. If you wanna dress like Mr. Peanut, then we're gonna treat you like Mr. Peanut! Don't you see? Peanuts are killing Americans twice as much as terrorism. Let's start defending ourselves NOW before the smoking gun comes in the shape of a Reese's Cup!

Four Degrees Removed From Reality

http://youtu.be/8KiRYuznNl0

I've got a game for you. It's fun. It's even more fun than "Six Degrees of Kevin Bacon." How often are you doing something that's removed from *actual* reality? Texting, tweeting, Facebooking, Skyping, watching TV — a lot, right? You know because sending a text is not actually speaking to someone. When you watch a porn, you're not actually fucking someone. When you pilot a drone aircraft, you're not actually flying bomber missions. When you watch Jay Leno, you're not actually laughing. And when you play Farmville 12 hours a day, you're not actually farming, but you ARE actually a fucking waste of flesh and hair.

So the game I've come up with is to play "Four Degrees of Separation From Reality." During your everyday activities, you point out the times when you're four or more steps removed from real life. Each day, the person with the most wins a car or something. (I haven't worked out the prize system yet.) For example, if you're currently watching this rant as a video, then you are only three steps removed from reality:

1) It's a video
2) It's on YouTube rather than a live video feed, and
3) It's made to look drawn rather than looking real.

Another example, if you describe to someone a Facebook photo you saw of a guy painting a woman masturbating, that's four degrees. If the person you talk to then twitters about your description, the world ends.

150

So much of our lives is removed from reality. Sometimes we just need to be here, now. And I'm not saying it's all bad. Getting videos out to people is crucial. It allows us to show police brutality or protests or chubby babies confused by their own ridiculous chubby cheeks. Those videos are crucial. But sometimes we are WAY overdoing it! Sometimes you should just fucking CALL SOMEONE. Don't tag them on a blog that connects to your twitter telling them that you emailed them about the text that you photocopied and had tattooed on your ass. Just FUCKING CALL THEM! Sometimes you don't have to take a photo and tag it on Facebook. Sometimes experiences are the end in and of themselves. Sometimes you don't need to paint that person masturbating. You could just enjoy it in the moment. Sometimes you can just eat a breakfast without Tweeting, "Why does my toast always burn when I'm watching it, and not when I'm not watching it! IRONIC!" First of all, NO, it's not ironic. It's just stupid. And secondly, you could've enjoyed that thought all by yourself.

And if you're wondering about reality shows... you've got people on television acting like they're not on television while simultaneously acting like they're not acting, written by writers, and then creatively cut together to create a story arch that never even happened. That's at least 12 degrees removed from anything that will ever be relevant to a human brain. ...which is the name of the new TLC reality show starring Kate Gosselin, Paris Hilton, and a spatula.

Are We The New Pompeii?

http://youtu.be/q1LFFbMMTsl

I was watching a documentary on Pompeii — the city in Rome that was completely covered by volcanic ash thousands of years ago, making it a sight to behold for excited tourists and overwhelmed chimney sweeps. We now know that the people of Pompeii were warned of the impending disaster by huge earthquakes that hit the city. Many people left but some stayed. What could be so important that some would stay in a collapsing city? Well, some of the bones found recently are permanently dyed green by a chemical reaction between the bones and... gold. These people were clutching huge amounts of gold when they gasped their final breath. As the world crashed and burned around them, many only feared for their jewelry.

So you gotta ask yourself: Are *we* there yet? As our society violently realizes it can't continue down this path, are we going to simply cling to our gold? And we do know it's slowly ending. We've felt the economic earthquakes. Even if you've been denying it, somewhere deep down you know this system is not sustainable. When you see a man shiver on a street corner while being passed by a dog wearing a turtleneck, you know this isn't sustainable. When you hear the US has the most obese people in the world and the most anorexic people in the world at the same fucking time, you know things aren't normal. When you read in *Us Weekly* that the sexiest woman in the world is struggling with cellulite problems, you know things aren't kosher. Why would God do that to her? When you see a stat that says we export 11 million tons of beef and veal and import 11 million tons of beef and veal, you know this doesn't make any common sense. I want to start a program called "Everybody just hang on to your fucking beef and veal. You keep yours. We'll keep ours. Save a lot of time and money."

So, are we going to koala bear ourselves onto a pile of gold as the ship goes down? Staining our bones green forever more? Future peoples and future species will dig us up and go, "Wow, they really liked certain kinds of rocks. This one mineral in particular appears to be more important than their friends, their families, their very existence. That musta been some fucking rock. God damn it! I wish we had rocks like that. I bet those rocks give unconditional love, and compliment your hair, and give you blow jobs and do the dishes. All at once! If I had a stone like that I would take it into the afterlife with me too. Mother Fucker!"

Or if you believe in a god and an afterlife, maybe that's why you're permanently dyed green. So in the afterlife everyone can know who the greedy bastards are — like a scarlet letter or an exploding dye pack in a bank robbery. After this world all the bankers and politicians and CEOs are dyed green so they can be ostracized and treated like second-class citizens. Signs at restaurants saying, "No greens allowed." They'd be denied jobs and apartments and loans simply based on the color of their bones. Now THAT is one afterlife I could believe in!

How To Decrease Corporate Power
Once And For All

http://youtu.be/_Yz48pm4ubc

You wanna really take the power away from the biggest corp-orations? You wanna REALLY punch them in the dick and shit in their punch bowl? Then follow this tried and true plan of action: STOP BUYING SO MUCH SHIT!! Stop it! Just stop IT. Every time you buy a thing, a trinket, a widget, or a custom-designed whatchamacallit, you give them a little more power and a little more money. The moment you stop, they flip the fuck out like a redneck on Jeopardy or a Kim Kardashian at a talent contest or an Indonesian 6-year-old NIKE employee listening to an American 6-year-old whine about how hard his homework is or Thomas Paine at a present-day Tea Party rally going, "Why the fuck are you wearing those ridiculous hats?!" They will flip THE FUCK OUT!

The reason our economy keeps trucking along while Americans can't find work and our social safety net has holes in it bigger than the ones in Rick Perry's logic is because we all keep buying stupid vapid shit and fighting each other for large TVs and preposterous houses. The moment we put down the iPads and Xboxes and pocket rockets, the large corporations would feel the pinch. We all know the expression "Vote with your wallet," but we need to vote by putting down our wallets. Cutting up our credit cards. Making do with the hordes of crap we already have. Give your kids a cardboard box for Christmas. Draw an X on it and tell them it's an Xbox. Kids are stupid. They'll believe anything. And if nothing else, it will prepare them for being homeless in 15 years if we don't change our current path.

My Calm and Collected Assessment Of The GOP Field

http://youtu.be/9ewAas2YN7c

I'm not going to say the left wing in this country is producing a lot of great leaders. But if you're a Republican right now, I feel bad for you. It's painful watching these debates with this flock of lizard-brained lizard-skinned beady-eyed half-wits. These multimillionaire pass-the-ammunition faux-Christian wrong-headed orange-headed dick-headed ego-maniacal evangelical twats who seem to lose every political debate to their arch nemesis: science. They have the same opinions on everything except who destroyed health care the best and who came out the strongest against helping old people afford their assisted living. This gaggle of bobble-headed giggle shits. These pretend-cowboys who are rugged and tough and manly and covered in more makeup than Christina Aguilera starring in Cirque Du Soleil. This is Ronald Reagan meets Ronald McDonald and fucks him in the ear hole until he drools Trickle Down theory. Each of them competing to be the next warmonger, itching to get their itchy trigger finger on the trigger. Hoping they can convince enough people that their lord, their imaginary anti-science, pro-life, pro-death penalty, pro-unmanned drone aircraft bombing, anti-drug, pro-alcohol, pro-money, anti-empathy, anti-gay, pro-materialism, anti-immigrant, pro-economic cannibalism LORD wants them to vote for this particular disingenuous clown over that disingenuous clown.

And there's nothing I hate more than a clown who's not straightforward with you. This fucking insane asylum of mentally ill, maniacally shrill oompa loompas all climbing on top of one another like a box of racist puppy dogs vying for your attention so they can convince you to believe the historically inaccurate portrait of President Reagan they've created out of duct tape, white-out, and anecdotes ripped from the pages of Spider Man. They don't believe in evolution, but if I were on that stage with that many backward-thinking cross-eyed Wal-Mart greeters, neither would I. Once Newt Gingrich is hunched over eating his scabs and Rick Santorum is trying to wipe his ass on a handicapped octogenarian in the front row, you TOO would question how advanced mankind is.

They are nothing more than tainted maggot-riddled flesh wrapped tightly around corporate donations telling you they can save America. They spend the commercial breaks filing down their ever-growing vampire teeth, still red from whichever state economy they last sucked dry. If their empty eyes seem a little watery, it's from the mace that Mother Nature sprayed into their faces as they tried to drill into every last crevice. But luckily they've pretty much developed immunity to mace. See, and who says they don't evolve?

Anyway, I just thought I would give you a short rundown of the Republican field. Should be a lively campaign season.

The Police Are On The Wrong Side
Of Occupy Wall Street

http://youtu.be/8mIZszPyK78

The Occupy Wall Street protest started this week, and I've been down there several times so far. And I realize the police are just doing their jobs, but there must be a little voice in each one of their heads telling him or her that it might make more sense to monitor and arrest the bankers and traders and economic rapers making millions while that policeman loses his benefits, loses his house, gets shot at for less and less money each year, gets vomited on by homeless alcoholics for less and less money each year, gets rubbed on by lonesome exhibitionists for less and less money each year. Instead, that policeman is beating down a 19-year-old with a feather in her hair and a henna tattoo because she had the nerve to draw in chalk on the sidewalk a message that reads, "Less money to create smart bombs and more money to create smart kids." As he's punching her in the head and screaming "Put the fuchsia chalk down! Step away from the chalk!" while wrenching her arms behind her back, there's gotta be a part of him thinking, "Wow, I just pawned my grandma's wedding ring so that I could afford to put my kid in day care so my wife could work a second job so her father could get the proper care for his Alzheimer's, and it was necessary because Wall Street has sucked this nation dry. But here I am right now putting a chokehold on a teenager because she won't put down the FUCKING CHALK! Maybe my priorities are a little out of whack."

They've been told to arrest peaceful protesters because chalk or signs or speeches through bullhorns might disrupt our fragile social order. But foreclosing on millions of families doesn't disrupt the social order?! Sending every job overseas doesn't disrupt the social order? Taking money out of infrastructure and putting it in tax cuts for millionaires doesn't disrupt the social order? We've got collapsing flood levees and bridge buttresses, people are floating by on old mattresses but those chalk messages, THOSE might truly cause pandemonium. If only we could somehow trick corporate heads and bankers into drawing something in chalk on the pavement or blocking an intersection or chanting through a bullhorn — maybe then we could finally FINALLY get them arrested. That's all it would take. Maybe if it's catchy enough, they would join in. Some chant like, "Go ahead and call us twats, we have credit default swaps!" Maybe then the police would have a reason to arrest those dick rags rather than imprisoning the vegan kid using arts and crafts to try to save the world.

But no, we live in a world where not only is greed good, it's enforced by law. Lacking in selfishness is a sin so scary, so threatening to the status quo that the powerful need riot cops and black ops to silence it.

The TRUTH About Occupy Wall Street

http://youtu.be/E9BKKr_CAAl

The Occupy Wall Street protest started something that is spreading across this country like a wave at a football stadium or a rash at a nudist colony. This movement started small & weird but has gotten strong & angry like Carrot Top did. Slowly people are realizing that it's okay to stand up, to raise their hand in solidarity. People are realizing that cops can't arrest everyone; they can't mace everyone; they can't take their daddy issues out on everyone. People are realizing it's okay to say that you too want corporations & millionaires to pay their fair share rather than devouring this country's resources, sucking it dry, leeching its life force. It's the economic version of a competitive eating competition — tremendously rotund corporations shoving hot dogs into their engorged, lying faces, hoping they won't vomit everywhere before the clock runs out. Trying to get one more hot dog, just ONE MORE BITE, and until now, no one has been stopping it. We've just been watching this morbid obesity with morbid curiosity going, "Are they really going to eat all that?? They can't possibly still be hungry. Why are they still eating at this point? I'VE NEVER SEEN ANYTHING LIKE IT!"

This is not a right or left issue. This is a right or wrong issue. Whoever's not willing to push for regulation and taxation of Wall Street is the enemy, whether left or right, black or white, male or female, dumb or old, whether politically aware or someone who paid money to see "Transformers 3"… or 2 …or 1… or anything by Michael Bay. *Anything.*

160

A lot has been made about the fact that a large percentage of the Occupy Wall Street protestors are young people and therefore aren't representative of America. Well, who the fuck do you think has the most to lose once this country looks like "The Day After Tomorrow" meets "The Day After?" Who do you think is dying overseas for a war that is now only about making Afghanistan safe for KBR shareholder profits? Who do you think has the most years left to breathe the polluted air, drink the tainted water, eat the mutated fish, and watch the fetid reality shit on TV that is clearly creating a nation of malignant imaginations?

We're the ones who have to sit in this rancid bath water twiddling our thumbs and flicking our ding-dongs for the next 70 years going, "Remember back when we coulda stopped this? Man, we shoulda, like, done something." So it started as young people. But now all brands of people are coming along. All ages, races, and creeds... Well, not those who *like* Creed. You're not welcome. But everyone else. Go to OccupyTogether.org & learn about the protests going on all over the country. There's one near you. You have no excuse. The powerful are not going to cede their money, their control, their debt enslavement reigns, their gold-plated toilet bowls without a fight, and we're only in round one.

But that's okay. I understand if you have better things to do than decide the future of this country. There's gotta be a Michael Bay movie on somewhere.

Stop Thinking Positively!

http://youtu.be/JEYafHrvz5g

I've got a pretty upbeat message today: STOP THINKING POSITIVELY! Don't do that anymore! Just stop it! Or nothing will ever change! Positive thinking is fine when it's done in moderation, when it's like, "I'm gonna have a good day today," or "There's *no way* I'll back into that lamp post," or "I will *never* regret this tattoo of star Buffalo Bills running back OJ Simpson." Fine. No real harm done. But when people use positive thinking as a life philosophy, it's a fucking catastrophe. Here are some examples of *bad* positive thinking:

"I'm *sure* our politicians will find a solution to the impending economic collapse" — or

"We'll figure out an answer to global warming before the floods get to *MY* house" — or

"Corporations wouldn't keep doing something if they found out it was killing millions" — or the more general:

"I'm sure *someone's* looking into that."

I did some thorough research on this topic and discovered — NO, NO ONE is looking into that! NO ONE is handling that, NO ONE is on top of that and most surprisingly, 98% of Americans haven't even *heard* of that! And 35% of the people who do know about it, only know because they heard a joke about it on Jimmy Kimmel Live! So STOP thinking positively! Think negatively. Think that this world is not gonna right itself without major change. Think that if we don't consider the environment soon, your kids will be living on a floating archipelago of old plastic bottles, trying to figure out how to best cook Styrofoam to make it only bearably cancerous instead of instantly cancerous.

I know these aren't pleasant thoughts. They're not as exciting as thinking about Jeter's batting average or which trajectory of angry bird will most catch those green dudes by surprise. You know, because it's not just about knocking down the towers, sometimes it's about showing those green dudes something they haven't seen before.

But without thinking negatively, nothing gets done. If Martin Luther King Jr. had thought, "I'm sure Black people will get rights sooner or later" nothing would've happened. If Betsy Ross had thought, "I'm sure soldiers will be equally happy to salute an old blanket or a quilt" then you and I would be pledging allegiance to a soiled duvet at this very moment. If Pepé Le Pew had thought to himself, "I'm sure that fine young lady will let me know when she's ready for my advances," then we would've missed out on YEARS of HILARIOUS sexual assault. Positive thinking is the antithesis of progress, the anti-advancement; it's a vacation from innovation. You've probably heard of the book *The Secret*? Well, the dark secret of *The Secret* is that it's a book about how to never achieve anything.

So stop thinking positively. Be cynical. Be a cynical optimist if you want. View the glass as half full... of shit. Then we can change the world.

The Best Kind Of Manipulation

http://youtu.be/HgnBDYD1czs

You know the only time I enjoy advertisements? When some computer entity has decided that a specific commercial applies to the video I'm watching. You know, you're enjoying a video on trucks and then it's interrupted by a commercial for Chevrolet. Or you're watching some MTV show online, and it's interrupted by an ad for horse manure because the computer correctly deduced, "If you like MTV, then you'll also LOVE THIS!" Or you're watching a rerun of "19 Kids and Counting" online and then there's commercial for condoms or toys made in China with lead paint — you know, something to stem the tide.

Anyway, I love those ads because it is some almost-sentient computer correctly figuring who you are and then advertising to you personally. I mean, we've given away all our privacy — so why not have computers working overtime to figure out who I am as a person and then manipulate me? It's the American way! But I like it even more when the computer really fucks up. When I'm watching an online documentary about how Wal-Mart is like gonorrhea if gonorrhea were less friendly, and then in the middle of it the computer algorithm thinks, "Oh, you like Wal-Mart?? Here's a Wal-Mart ad! Yay!" I love those moments because Wal-Mart is FUCKING PAYING for that shit! I just stole two dollars from Wal-Mart and that makes me happy. Or I'm watching something on how hydraulic fracking is slightly more evil than Skeletor but slightly less evil than Timothy Geithner, and right then, an ad pops up with an Exxon

Mobil spokesperson happily informing me that fracking is wonderful because it makes your tap water flammable, which cuts your Crème Brûlée cooking time in half!! HALF, I tell you!

Or, I'm watching something on the BP oil spill, and then I get a commercial for Astro-Glide. And I'm like, "Not THAT kind of oil! Dumb computer! If BP had spilt THAT kind of oil in the Gulf of Mexico the wild life would be having a massive beach-wide orgy with turtles and birds and raccoons all going at it — kinda how I envision Ted Nugent's house except with less Ted Nugent. And anything with less Ted Nugent is better.

Anyway, point being our computer overlords don't have us figured out quite yet. We have at least a year or two left of hilarious commercials before they finally nail down the formula and begin farming us for energy. Like that movie with Keanu Reeves where he's like "What's going on? What? Whoahhh? What? Whoahhh." I think it was called "Bill & Ted's Robot Adventure."

Wall Street Is Dirtier
Than Occupy Wall Street

http://youtu.be/ClbiGR75nqY

Back during the initial Wisconsin protests against Governor Walker I discussed how the protesters were being called "dirty" or "unclean." And now here we are again — the same attack on courageous protesters demonstrating what democracy really looks like. How is it that this same attack could be used so regularly? Well, the systemic breaking down of protest movements by the powerful and the mindless is not new, and they're using the same tired playbook they've used for ages. The media has some sort of Tourette's Syndrome where they immediately call protesters dirty. And I'm going to say the same thing I said months ago: the funny thing about protesting the dismantling of our society by the greedy and the fake-tanned is that it hardly ever happens near a 24-hour drycleaner and an exfoliation station. It's almost never in someone's living room over wine and cheese with your shoes off so as to not sully the carpet or the Labradoodle.

We're out there because what we're protesting for is more important than a daily shower with fragrant shower gel and a light shampoo ball wax in the morning. And it's even more important than — wait for it — money! Because most of us are not out there because we don't have a job. We're out there because our generation and our species don't have a future if we continue down this path.

But still, we're called slobs. By this definition you know who else were slobs? The soldiers in World War II: I heard they slept in the mud! The astronauts: I hear they almost never shower or have a Swedish dry skin treatment for as much as a month! The civil rights protesters: I heard they bled on each other without bathing. The only reason they got cleaned off was because considerate, racist citizens and police officers saw that they were slobs and turned fire hoses on them. It was a compassionate power-washing of the people.

In fact, I'd go as far as to say that almost everything great and noble and impassioned that's ever happened in this country has happened while dirty. People rescuing neighbors after hurricane Katrina— filthy. MLK Jr. during his "I have a dream" speech — grimy from marching. JFK while banging Marilyn Monroe — sticky. George W. Bush forging his way through "My Pet Goat" despite obstacles as immense as an attack on this country — covered in flop sweat.

So everybody worried that the protesters are dirty, I suggest you grab a Sham-Wow and some Oxy-Clean because we're spilling our blood, sweat, and tears to try to salvage this democracy from political hypocrisy and corporate sodomy and scrubbing behind our ears isn't at the top of our fucking list at the moment.

The Numbers Behind Occupy Wall Street

http://youtu.be/4Adr_Pck6Vl

I'm not normally the guy who brings you numbers. I bring you bitching. But in the interest of proof, here are some numbers to explain why the 99% are standing up in New York, and Denver, DC, and San Francisco, and London, Boston, Montreal and Madison and about 2,000 other cities around the globe.

In the 1970's the top one percent took in 8-9 % of America's total annual income. Today they suck in 23.5%, according to TruthOut. org. Ten percent of Americans devour almost 50% of all wages — which is greater than any year since 1917 — according to Berkeley Professor Emmanuel Saez. Do you have any idea how long ago that was? They were still using expressions like "She's the bees' knees" back then! Seventy-four of the richest people in the US get paid $10 million a week, which taken together is as much as 19 million of the lowest-paid people in America. That's from *The Huffington Post*. Net worth of the richest Americans is $1.5 trillion, more than the combined net worth of the poorest 50% of the entire population, which is 155 million people combined — that's from Truth Out. The top 1% of the population owns 70% of all assets, an all-time record — according to David Degraw. The top one also have over 85% of the world's biggest assholes, according to me. But according to Fox News the bottom 50% of this country is queer.

So you can see, it's all in the numbers. The wealth of this country is being increasingly pulled to a very few individuals at the top. And as we know from simple physics, things that are incredibly top-heavy collapse. All you have to do is think back to the 2003 Oscars when James Gandolfini rode on Natalie Portman's shoulders down the red carpet. The awards show was ultimately canceled so that construction crews could dig Portman out of the pavement.

And for those you who argue that it benefits America to have hugely successful corporations, they aren't going to stay here once they've EATEN EVERYTHING! I think Dylan Rattigan put it best on MSNBC when he said America is being extracted, while WE all sit around distracted by petty political squabbling. America's resources are being sucked out of it like a ping-pong ball into a Thai Lady Boy. And it's happening to a lot of other countries too because corporations and those who run them have no moral code or alle-giance outside of money. They never think they should behave a certain way because it's good for the country or good for the people. They don't say the pledge of allegiance before they lay off 10,000 workers or eat apple pie before purchasing 100,000 acres in Utah to clear-cut. They don't have a big foam finger that says "USA is #1" on it, and if they do, it says "Dubai is #1" on the reverse side in case they need to pick up and move at a moment's notice. The ultra-rich in Mexico don't have sombreros that say "Mexico rocks," and the corporations in England don't wear tee shirts that say "God save the Queen." Instead they say "God save the green." (And for those of you thinking "But their money isn't green," FUCK YOU! I had to make the joke work! "God the save the pinky-purple bits of paper" DOESN'T HAVE THE SAME RING TO IT, DOES IT?!)

We have created absolute monsters that are sucking all remaining wealth and resources from our land. Some of 'em don't even create anything. They just suck and suck and suck like Eddie Murphy movies. These corporations haven't been good in any way since the late 1980's, like Eddie Murphy. So at least think about these facts when the media is telling you how fucking furious you should be that the Occupy Wall Street protesters in your area are holding up a big sign with a curse word on it.

It's Time To Pull America
Out Of The Stone Age

http://youtu.be/j_ALAkUATwI

We think we have the right to avenge a death, by deciding life and death, choosing the time of a last breath. But the breadth of the situation, mindless retaliation, runs deep in our country's psyche, its Freudian aggravation. We consider it a God-given right to decide that God's not right to keep this man alive. His life is God's oversight. But whose god? Yours or mine? Which god? The diamond one around your neck or the one in your mind? In this blood sport of lethal injection, there's no mental reflection, no legal objection. There's only disconnection of institutions all morally absolving themselves of the final solution. If we're gonna kill as regular practice, let's at least make it entertaining, fun for the whole family. Execute people randomly, put it on national TV, hosted by Britney or Bristol or some other intellectual lobotomy. Maybe fireworks attached to the electric chair. If it's not fair, at least there should be some flare, some singed hair and fan fair! Something to make fans stare and gasp and gawk and gag and maybe then reflect on why we had the gag reflex and how it reflects on our nation that we still partake in this abomination.

Why Don't The Occupy Protesters Stop Whining And Just Work Hard?

http://youtu.be/s3cOOyHuwv0

Something I hear from right-wingers — whether it be a friend of mine or Herman Cain or Mumm-Ra — something I hear is, "Why don't the protesters stop complaining and just work hard? I believe in hard work. Why don't people just shut up and work hard?" And here's the thing they seem to be overlooking — these people ARE working hard. Most Americans are working REALLY fucking hard. There's a lot of hard-working janitors and teachers, nurses and cashiers, secretaries and fluffers, librarians and sheet metal cutters, sound technicians and lab technicians, black jack dealers and drug dealers, bodega rat chasers and cake bakers, cable repairmen, naval airmen, and wax-your-back-hair men. And EVERY ONE of them is working really fucking hard and MOST aren't making much money and aren't living easy lives. Hard work only equals hundreds of thousands of dollars in a few select professions.

The point is we, as a wealthy country, should have a society where if you work hard in ANY profession, you can have a happy life. We have the resources. They're all right there in front of us. So I don't care if you have the worst job in the world. I don't care if your job is cleaning turds out of the corner of the turd factory — if you work full time, you should be able to feed and clothe your kids! First of all, it's the moral thing do to. Secondly, with the size of our kids, none of us want to see them half-clothed! None of us want to see a 10-year-old boy's TITS bouncing up and down on a sweaty summer day! Can't we get together as a country and buy that boy some pasties? A set of shiny new nipple tassels? And I realize Bill O'Reilly will call them socialist nipple tassels, but who gives a shit? I'd rather have socialist nipple tassels than capitalist boy boobs in my face! Wouldn't you?!

And that's what the Occupy movement is about... kinda. Occupy Wall Street's not saying people shouldn't work. It's saying if people work hard in whichever profession they choose, the game shouldn't be rigged against them so that their pension is circumcised a year before they retire in order to give the CEO a bigger, thicker, longer-lasting bonus! Enough with the enormous, throbbing bonuses! They're unseemly!

Occupy Wall Street Has Proven
We Don't Have Free Speech

http://youtu.be/JFWSDSovKdg

We claim to live in a land of free speech. We cherish that right. We love it and cling to it like Pastor Fred Phelps to his secret stash of gay porn. We rub it in the face of other countries: "Look at us, you motherfuckin' ass wipes! We have free speech! We can call you 'motherfuckin ass wipes' if we want to... And WE WANT TO!"

We love our free speech... except when we don't. Except when it's more than five people at once or after 10pm or amplified by a microphone or megaphone or near a building that contains men with suit pants or women with pant suits or when it's on a sidewalk or on a holiday or near tents or when the message being conveyed is disagreeable to people drinking a fine wine. Other than those times, enjoy your free speech! If you happen to break one of those rules, then we'll kindly present you with a gift: It's a tear gas canister, and it will be coming toward you at an impressive speed! Doesn't matter if you're one of the soldiers who fought overseas to ensure those rights. We'll still pummel you if you proceed.

I have a deal to make with the ruling elite. If you want to crack down on our free speech when it's a message you disagree with — fine. BUT in return we, the people, reserve the right to take away free speech when it's a message *we* disagree with. For example, CNN's House of Brain-Dead News or Tyler Perry's House of Payneful Comedy or MTV's Summer House of Walking STD's. We reserve the right to fire pepper spray at them or to duct tape the mouths of Presidential candidates talking in circles about nonsense caked in affable hand gestures.

Or ex-military military analysts who spent 20 years bombing other countries and now want to let the American people know that the answer to their problems is—GASP—to bomb other countries. Doesn't matter what the problem is. Iran tests a missile? Bomb something. Pirates off Somalia? Bomb something. "Deal or No Deal" dropping in ratings? Bomb something. Europe criticizing our tendency to bomb at the drop of a hat? Bomb something.

Where are the peace analysts on CNN or NBC? Where are the guys who spent 20 years in the peace trenches waging peace, bringing peace to areas of the world that had never seen it before... like the Pentagon? If you're going to hire blow-things-up experts to tell us to blow things up, then at least also hire peace experts to say that idea fucking blows!

CEOs And Pedophiles/
Corporate Greed And Touching Children

http://youtu.be/doeF-p5-Rn8

It came out last week that the Canadian Boy Scouts have had thousands of cases of child molestation over the past 40 years. The reporter I saw made an interesting point — that jobs like being a scoutmaster tend to attract pedophiles because they have easy access to children. It's much more difficult to ask a kid to go camping in the woods alone with you if you're a 45 yr-old man *without* a funny uniform and some badges that say you know how to knit. Other jobs also attract these sleazeballs, such as gym coach, priest, birthday party clown, or puppet. And I'm not saying all the people in those professions are pedophiles, only that those positions ATTRACT pedophiles. You know, for every 12 Kermit the Frogs you get, you're gonna attract one Snuffleupagus.

Similarly, I rail against the sickening greed of big CEOs a lot. And there's a reason most CEOs make decisions that your average human being couldn't stomach. Think about the type of people that job attracts. Think about who rises all the way up the ranks at a corporation. It's certainly NOT the guy who cares the most about workers benefits or about the last 12 square feet of territory the spotted owl is hanging onto. It's not the vegetarian who lets people merge in front of him on the highway. It's not the guy who thinks the meaning of life is to live in the moment and enjoy our shared humanity and turns off his cell phone every weekend so as to get in touch with his spirit animal. Nope. The guys or girls who rise to the top of a massive corporation are the ones who put profit above all else — above American jobs and workers' health, above the environment and WAY above their spirit animals. No one ever got promoted at a huge corporation because they figured out how to get slightly more expensive materials made by proud, hard-working American adults instead of Chinese toddlers. These people get promoted because they find a way to save the company a few million dollars a year by laying off the workers who are most likely to complain about their cancer instead of sucking it up and walking it off.

So this means the men and women who end up running the big corporations, the men and women who are some of the most powerful people in the world are FUCKING PSYCHOPATHS! Greedy, hungry, nasty psychopaths! THAT's who scores that job! The job attracts those type of people like a moth to a flame, like a former child star to a rehab, like an obese 10-year-old to a kiosk with fried Oreos, like a 21-year-old girl on her birthday to a bathroom floor. Okay, I'm exaggerating — only 90% of CEOs are psychopaths. The others are just run-of-the-mill standard-issue plain-vanilla assholes!

How To Rig An Election
In Just A Few Easy Steps

http://youtu.be/TzCx6F5oSxc

If there is one thing that's at the center our country's being, at the core of our essence, like the tarnished and singed gold coins that make up Alan Greenspan's soul, it's our belief in voting: one man, one vote. It's the heart of our democracy. You take away our free and fair elections and we don't have a whole lot else to show ya. It's kinda like if Hooters declared they were going to replace their top-heavy waitresses with senior citizens on Rascal scooters. Sure, you could still enjoy the fucking chicken wings, but no one would be dying to go there on a Friday night.

And that's why we should all give a shit that in the 2012 election we will have NO IDEA who won. It could be Obama; it could Mitt Romney; it could be Ron Paul's nipple hairs. You won't know. You won't fucking know.! Ninety percent of the votes cast in 2012 will be counted in secret by computers programmed by a few corporations with ties to extremist political and religious groups. And the funny thing is, if this were a sporting event instead of a presidential election, the country WOULD NEVER stand for it. Just imagine if officials announced that the last five minutes of the World Series would be played at a black site in Pakistan with no video and no reporters. All the nutty fans would be chloroformed, and all the deranged announcers would be rounded up and shot. Okay, that doesn't sound like a bad thing in and of itself, but seriously, imagine if they did that. Or if they decided the Super Bowl in secret, and then an old guy walked out and said, "Trust me, the Detroit Lions won." The country would go Gary Busey-in-line-for-five-hours-at-the-DMV crazy! Bricks through windows, riots in the streets! Occupy Wall Street would look like a Pilates retreat. It would be fucking chaos. If it were a NASCAR event decided at a top-secret facility, hicks and rednecks would storm the gates and hurl goats at the owners... or whatever it is rednecks do when they're mad.

But when it comes to our elections, we seem to be okay with a faith-based system. We'll take your word on this one. Big corporations have lied to us every step of the way, but we'll trust them to be kind to the core of our democracy. This is like that guy ripping out that dude's still-beating heart in "Indiana Jones." And rather than fighting to take our heart back, we've said to the man who's laughing like Charlie Manson watching Deer Hunter, "Okay, you can borrow it. But just take good care of it."

And even if we did trust those companies for some reason, we have more to worry about than just them. Bev Harris at **black-boxvoting.org** hacked into a Diebold ballot counter with a monkey... I'm not kidding... There's video... Google it. So now anyone can fuck up our elections, even the animal kingdom. And don't think they don't want to. That animal kingdom has been gunning for us for ages. Remember that killer whale that ate that person a few years back?? Yeah, I rest my case.

There *are* ways to fix this. The easiest one is a new technology developed by the smartest minds at MIT. It allows every single man & woman to cast a vote that can be observed by all and counted in public. So even if there is fraud, the fraud can be discovered and fixed. This new device is as light as a piece of paper and as easy to use as a pencil. And most importantly, can't be hacked by foreign governments or anarchist squirrels. We need to insist that EVERY election use THIS DEVICE. It's called... paper. IT'S PAPER! We should use PAPER! PAPER BALLOTS, GODDAMMIT! And I know what you're thinking, "Paper? Isn't that the thing I wipe my ass with? That sounds repulsive!" Yes, but that's a different kind of paper. That's tissue paper. This other type of paper will allow us to actually stop corporations and right-wing lunatics from wiping their asses with our democracy. And we can fix that chad problem we had a few years back. I knew a Chad in high school, and *anyone* could kick his ass. Besides this may be the only way to stop the kitten-alliance in this country from hacking into our voting machines and placing their own kitten leader into the presidency. And you'll wish you stopped this shit when you're watching CNN and you see written across the bottom of the screen, "Can I haz presidency? Mr. Snickers-face is the new President Elect of the United States of America."

Afraid To Stand Up Against Your Corporate Oppressors? Try Some Occupy!

http://youtu.be/G9yENsvSMhM

Look, I get it. You don't wanna stand up for the Occupy movement because you've cared about things in the past and they've always ended up sucking. You voted for this guy or campaigned for that guy, and then it turned out this guy was a little boy enthusiast — to use a euphemism — and THAT guy voted to turn your local park system into an Indian-casino-slash-oil-pipeline called "Sticky Bear." I get it! You're like, "Fuck this! Changing things *never* works. I'm gonna go back to playing 'Grand Theft Auto' where my actions actually matter. If I shoot a grandma in the face, she dies. End of story. No one walks in and goes, 'Oh, we recounted the votes and she didn't die.'"

I get it. It's called "learned helplessness," and it makes people depressed and apathetic. In one study done on dogs they found that a dog that was shocked for a specific action he could learn to expect was far happier than a dog shocked periodically for no reason. The random-shocks dog became depressed and lethargic because it had developed learned helplessness. And no, I don't know where the fuck PETA was during the study, and no, I don't know why the experimenters didn't use a far less-loved animal, like an anti-Semitic pigeon or an Elisabeth Hasselbeck. Nobody cares about those. We as citizens have been periodically shocked for no reason by corporate decisions. They take away your health care. They take away your pension. They take away your job. They cancel "Arrested Development." Then you're touched by the bad men at airport security. The indignities never cease! And we are now that lonely dog, depressed, apathetic and just waiting for the next shock, thinking there's nothing we can do except lick our crotch and wait.

But Occupy is different, and it's time to stand up and dust ourselves off. As author Bruce Levin says in his recent book, we're in an abusive relationship with the corporatocracy and step one is to regain our self respect. So all of you saying Occupy won't change anything, I want you to know, it's okay to walk out that door. You can find another man, a good man who will say thank you and do the dishes sometimes and go down on you without acting like it's a chore, and not steal your dental care in the middle of the night. You know, a *good* man! You can do it. You can stand up and join us! This movement is different because it's not based around a tired, old political party funded by the same people who are abusing you. This movement is powered by all the other abuse victims. There are roughly 300 million of us, and it's time we sought out a new relationship. And besides, I hear Goldman Sachs has a small dick anyway.

Kim Kardashian, Occupy Wall Street, And Credit Default Swaps

http://youtu.be/LL36f08pnUA

Kim Kardashian. Kim Kardashian. *Kim Kardashian* **Kim Kardashian!!** There, now do I have your attention? It's just a fact that certain types of topics are sexy, attractive, grab people's attention and focus and won't let go — like silly celebrities, devastating hurricanes, fiery crashes that involve a clown car colliding into an ice cream stand and a petroleum truck, exploding into a rainbow of tragic, yet colorful, pieces. *Those* make for sexy news stories. *Those* are sensational and easy to talk about. The scams and criminals that have nearly destroyed our society on the other hand, more complicated. They can't be relayed in fucking sound bites. Subprime mortgages, derivatives, credit default swaps, and the Federal Reserve don't have the requisite tanned tits or ripped athletes, building collapses or celebrity relapses to get talked about on a regular basis. Not only do they not get reported on, those topics haven't even been discussed in the presidential debates. How extensively has Rick Perry talked about fractional reserve banking? He's talked about it only slightly less than he's discussed his upcoming plans for Chanukah, the Jewish festival of lights.

The men and women sitting at the table of the financial markets around the world and extracting all the wealth, wreaking havoc on average people, rely on the fact that we won't want to talk about complicated issues when we're getting our hair cut or standing at a urinal trough with seven other men. We'll talk about weather, and sports, and maybe, if we want to raise the level of conversation, we'll shift to how the nachos seem to be giving us gas, but that's where it ends. They know we won't sit through a news story on credit default swaps, but we WILL sit through one on an ostrich that escaped from the zoo and is causing mayhem at a nearby elementary school. The chubby kids can't outrun an ostrich!! What will we do?!

They rely on the fact that we won't riot to stop the grandest theft in a thousand years, but we will instead riot over things like the dismissal of a football coach who was protecting a child rapist.

And we all know the media long ago gave up on their responsibility to report the news. They report whatever the highest number of people will sit and watch. And that's why Occupy Wall Street scares the shit out of them. It's changing the conversational paradigm in this country. More people know what corporate personhood and Citizens United are than ever before. Income inequality and corporate greed are dinner table topics now. And we didn't even have to blow up a truck full of clowns to do it..... I mean, we did blow up a truck full of clowns, but it was purely for sport.

You Can't Pepper Spray
A Mental Awakening!

http://youtu.be/dX3mb67Hyns

So here we are. You've arrested us, you've tear gassed us, you've barricaded and pepper sprayed us, but we're bigger, stronger, and more resolved than ever. Perhaps you should try hurling other shit at us — maybe banana pudding or babaganoush grenades. Maybe that will slow us down. Do you have any extra kitchen sinks? You could hurl kitchen sinks at us.

"Why are they still here?" you're probably wondering. "How is this happening?" Well, I'm feeling generous, so I'll tell you why. You're fighting on the ground level in a quaint, and to be honest, barbaric manner. But we're fighting from our souls and our minds. We've waging a revolution of thought, a battle of ideas, a war to drag this country's subconscious anger into conscious passion. YOU CAN'T PEPPER SPRAY A FUCKING THOUGHT! So stop trying! That shit stings, goddammit! But it doesn't slow us down. It just makes us angrier!... but it is fucking annoying. It's like if your opponent farts during an MMA fight. You're not gonna forfeit, but you'll be like, "Aw, come ON! Really?!"

Here, I'll put all this into easier terms for you. You know the most recent X-Men movie? I think it was called "X-Men: We're gonna keep making these until we're all dead!" Anyway, in that movie, Kevin Bacon plays a mutant who, whenever he gets hit by a missile, just absorbs the energy and gets stronger. But the US military only knows one solution to any problem, so they *keep* firing missiles. That's what you're doing. And it's just making us bigger. And coincidentally, Kevin Bacon in real life lost all his money in a Wall Street Ponzi scheme. Sound familiar? And coincidentally Kevin Bacon was also once told he couldn't dance. And he just danced and danced and danced until the corporate elite were like, "ALRIGHT! YOU CAN FUCKING DANCE!" So look into my eyes mayors, and senators, and representatives and corporate motherfuckers across this country — WE ARE KEVIN BACON!"

But really, if you wanna look at the perfect symbol of fighting two different types of battles, look at the metal barricades that now fully surround Liberty Plaza. Let me repeat that — metal barricades that surround LIBERTY plaza in the shadow of the FREEDOM tower. Billionaire Bloomberg thinks he can cordon off liberty and freedom. They're very scary ideas so we better surround them with these metal gates. We wouldn't want free speech just running rampant around the city.

Unfortunately, it doesn't work that way. You're trying to sweep up mercury with a broom. You're trying to punch a dream! You're trying to stop a raging river with a spider web! Don't you get it?

- You've got batons, but we've got ideas.
- You've got mace, but we've got memes.
- You've got false arrests, but we've got our convictions.
- You've got horses, but we've got cats... some of us... some of us have cats.
- You've got handcuffs, but we've got the energy of generations of steadily increasing abuse.
- You're driven by hatred and your true bosses by greed, but we're driven by the possibility of a better world.
- You're fighting a war for the landscape, but we're fighting a war for the mindscape.

- We would welcome you on our side with open arms, otherwise you can just keep trying to teargas a mental awakening.

But it won't work because WE ARE... KEVIN BACON.

Occupy Wall Street
Is A Thought Revolution

http://youtu.be/WTHv4exE5el

The *New York Times* — the highly respected *New York Times* — did a great article yesterday about Occupy Wall Street. The entire report revolved around how Occupy Wall Street is a big pain in the ass to the area's public bathrooms. Now, there are two things you need to know about that last sentence: A) I'm not kidding. B) The double entendre was unintentional. There will be several more of those in the following few paragraphs and ALL of them are unintentional ...except for seven.

The *New York Times* — which is a so-called liberal media outlet — is more concerned with the harm done to the public restrooms than they are with the harm done to the America people by corporations and Wall Street titans who make Charlie Sheen's moral compass look like that of Harriet Tubman. As billionaires continue to shit all over this country like it's a bathroom near Occupy Wall Street, the media is more worried about the bathrooms near Occupy Wall

Street?? Are you FUCKING SERIOUS?! Get your head out of your ass and maybe you'll be able to better see your priorities! This world is a shit storm of greed that desperately needs mopping up. We're talking about people's homes, people's lives, people's dreams! And the media wants to make it about the discomfort of the millionaires who live around Zuccotti Park? The article said mothers have trouble getting strollers around police barricades. God forbid the revolution should get in the way of your evening stroll with little baby trust fund.

This may not be a revolution in the traditional sense, but this a revolution in thought. Americans are tired of greed over good, profitable pollution over people, war for wealth over the welfare of average workers. This is a thought revolution, and the revolution will not be sanitized. It will be criticized, ridiculed, misconstrued and misunderstood. But it will push through. Shit all over it all you want but the floodgates are open now!

The revolution will *not* be tidy. The revolution will *not* fit with your Pilates schedule. The revolution will *not* be quiet after 10pm, and it will not fit easily into a mainstream media-defined paradigm. The revolution will affect your bottom line. The revolution will affect you whether you ignore it or not. The revolution will not be dissuaded by barricades or pepper spray, driving rain, police rage, or ankle sprains. Pepper spraying us is like throwing water on gremlins — the more you do it, the more of us FUCKING SHOW UP! The revolution will be annoying to the top 1% and those who aren't open-minded enough to understand it. The revolution does not care if you satirize it; you still won't be able to jeopardize it. The revolution will not wait until after your hair appointment, dinner party, tummy tuck, or titty tilt. The revolution doesn't care about your lack of intellectual curiosity. The revolution will not be televised as Gil Scott-Heron told us, but it will be digitized and available on YouTube, Facebook, Twitter, and anywhere real ideas are told! You might have to wade through some invites for Farmville, but it'll be in there. The revolution will not be hijacked by your old, tired, rejected political beliefs. The revolution will not be monetized, commercialized, circumcised, or anesthetized. Good god — don't you get it? Greed is no longer good, and it's not God. And the thought revolution is here to stay whether you give two shits about it or not!

The revolution WOULD however like to apologize for shitting all over your apathy. Now pick a side.

*I would love to keep in touch with you. The Moment Of Clarity videos and podcast come out twice a week at **www.LeeCamp.net**. Please go there to watch, listen, and become a member. You can also follow me on Twitter: @LeeCamp as well as @NewsDecoder.*

*For a digital copy of this book in which you can click on the links, order **Moment Of Clarity** from Amazon Kindle, Smashwords, BarnesandNoble.com, Sony, Apple iBooks, and many other digital retail platforms. The **Moment Of Clarity** e-book is published in association with Fearless Books (www.fearlessbooks.com).*

15909340R00107

Made in the USA
Charleston, SC
26 November 2012